THRIFTY HOUSEHOLD

More than 1000 budget-friendly hints and tips

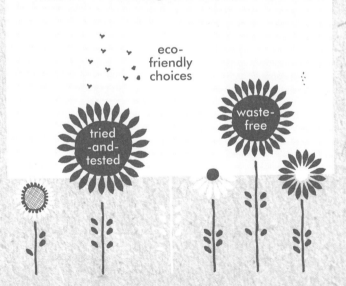

eco-friendly choices

tried-and-tested

waste-free

COLLECTED WISDOM FROM
THE COUNTRY WOMEN'S ASSOCIATION OF VICTORIA INC.

CONTENTS

INTRODUCTION

It is with much pleasure that we share these handy hints for a Thrifty Household with you.

The Country Women's Association of Victoria Inc. was formed in March 1928, during difficult times of drought, hardship, isolation, loneliness and lack of access to services that many of us now take for granted. Today, we continue to address issues affecting vulnerable women, children and our communities, and offer the hand of friendship and support to all women – both rural and urban.

The remedies, hints and solutions to household problems listed in these pages use mostly natural products. When The Country Women's Association of Victoria Inc. was formed, there weren't the commercial products available that we have access to now, neither were shops readily accessible to buy such products. By necessity, women and their families had to make do, repair and reuse. No food or produce was wasted. Excess fruit was preserved in jars or made into jams, and excess vegetables were turned into delicious pickles, sauces and chutneys. The skilful art of turning leftovers from one meal into the next tasty meal was much valued.

Skip forward to 2020 and we are all much more aware of how we need to look after our planet and use fewer harsh chemicals in favour of more natural products. It is coincidental that the old remedies also turn out to be more economical.

There has been an increase in interest by families wishing to grow at least some of the food they consume, as well as learning how to preserve excess produce. An appreciation for eating organic, nourishing food, and an awareness of the amount of food wasted each year, has families challenging themselves with the 'waste not, want not' ethos.

Within these pages you will also find ideas to save money and help the family budget by using natural ingredients to make some of your own beauty products.

Many people are becoming more concerned about disposability and the volume of waste we produce; with a little effort and help from the hints in this book, we can extend the life of our clothes and other household items.

How life has changed since 1928; but isn't it wonderful to know that natural products such as white vinegar, bicarbonate of soda and lemon juice are still as useful and relevant today as they were back then? We trust that this book will be the first one you reach for to find the answer to any Thrifty Household question.

Marion Dewar
State President

✦

Noela MacLeod AO
Member of Honour

KITCHEN

KITCHEN HINTS

+ White vinegar and eucalyptus oil are good general **disinfectants**.

+ Line your **kitchen bin** with three old supermarket bags. When one is full, the next one is already there, ready for use. Never again will your teenagers unseeingly drop their rubbish into an unlined bin while you're outside... taking out the rubbish.

+ To clean a **ceiling** stained with cooking steam, wash with hot water and laundry detergent.

+ To clean up **spilt honey** without leaving sticky traces, use a cloth dipped in salty water.

+ To enhance the flavour of old **herbs and spices**, pop them in the microwave for 30–40 seconds.

+ To restore a discoloured **wooden chopping board**, soak it overnight in a bowl of water with ½ cup bleach added. Next day, rinse well in very hot water, allow to dry completely, then sandpaper all over, including the edges. Rinse again in cold water.

+ If there isn't enough **bench space** in your kitchen at busy times, buy a chopping board big enough to fit over the sink to create more space. Alternatively, open a top drawer under the bench and rest a tray or pastry board on it.

+ Sew a magnet into the corner of a **pot-holder** so that it can be stored attached to the stove, easy to reach for whenever you need it.

+ You never see a chef use the **blade of a knife** to scrape food from the board into a pan. The knife is always turned onto the blunt side, so as not to dull the sharp edge.

+ To keep a **sharp knife** safely in your cutlery drawer, make a knife guard. Take the cardboard tube from inside a finished roll of kitchen towel, flatten one end and tape it closed.

+ When you wash Tupperware or other **storage containers**, dry them, then place half a piece of kitchen towel in each container before putting on the lid. The lid won't get lost and the towel soaks up any dampness, so the container stays fresh and dry in the drawer.

+ Before you start cooking, open your **cookbook** to the right page and slip it into a clear plastic bag. You can still read the recipe and the book is protected from any spills and splashes.

+ If you need quick and **easy recipes**, turn to a children's cookbook.

+ Squash kitchen towels and toilet rolls to an **oval shape** so they don't roll as easily. You will be surprised how much it helps reduce the amount used.

+ When you're **entertaining**, use bowls with suction seals on the bottom (sold for small children, or make your own). These are great for serving dips, as the bowl can't slide off the tray.

+ Before washing **valuable china** and crystal, always place a folded cloth at the bottom of the sink to prevent cracking and chipping.

+ Protect your **precious china** by slipping a paper plate between each piece as you stack it away.

+ To prevent large plastic bottles of **soft drink** losing all their fizz when they aren't finished, squeeze the bottle to exclude all the air before putting the lid on for storage.

+ Coffee is a good **air purifier**, so burn a little in a tin on top of the stove and any household smells will disappear.

+ To clean and freshen a **fridge**, dissolve 1 teaspoon bicarbonate of soda in a bowl of warm water, or just use the soda on a damp cloth. Wipe the fridge with this solution, then rinse and dry. Finish with white vinegar for a shine on the outside.

+ Keep a half-empty bottle of **champagne** bubbly by putting a teaspoon in the neck, handle down.

+ If you've forgotten to chill a **bottle of wine**, here's a quick solution. Wet a hand towel and wring it out. Wrap it around the wine bottle, put it in the freezer for 10 minutes and the wine will be chilled.

+ Keep an empty jam jar for storing **rubber bands**. The little ones can be placed inside and the big ones round the outside. It's much better than keeping them jumbled up in a drawer.

+ A soda siphon is a useful emergency **fire extinguisher** for any fire you would put out with water (but never an electrical fire or one caused by fat or burning oil).

+ Keep a packet of flour near your stove or barbecue. If **fat catches fire** while cooking, smother the flames quickly and safely with flour. It is messy, but effective.

+ You can use an ordinary glass bottle to sharpen **blunt scissors**. Use the scissors as if you were trying to cut off the neck of the bottle, and they'll end up with a sharp cutting edge.

+ To make a good-value, non-stick **cooking spray**, add 1 cup water to 3 cups cooking oil and store in a plastic spray bottle. Shake well before use.

+ Use warm water, rather than hot, to **clean glasses** that have held milk. Hot water 'bakes' the milk to the glass.

+ Laundry bleach cleans **tea stains** from cups. Add 2 tablespoons to a sink of water and soak the cups for 5 minutes. Then wash as usual.

+ Manual **can openers** work better if you run hot water over them before use.

+ If your **hands smell** of onions or fish, run them under cold water and rub with lemon juice before washing with soap.

+ If a knife has picked up a **fishy taste** or smell, plunge it into garden soil before washing.

+ Drain **fried food** on crumpled kitchen towel to absorb any oil.

+ To clean **painted cupboard doors**, use 1 tablespoon borax dissolved in boiling water to make soapy water.

+ Wooden fruit bowls and other **wooden tableware** should never be immersed in water. Instead, wipe out with a damp cloth after use. Occasionally, rub the wood lightly with a cloth dipped in vegetable oil to 'feed' the wood. Any bad stains or marks should be treated by rubbing gently with fine steel wool, rubbing along the grain only.

BENCHTOP

+ Mop up **benchtop spills** quickly – they can be absorbed by laminate within minutes. Dip a damp plastic scourer in bicarbonate of soda and use to wipe the benchtop. Wipe off with a damp cloth.

+ For particularly bad **marks**, make a paste of bicarbonate of soda and lemon juice and paint on; leave overnight and then rinse off the next day.

+ For **white laminate**, cover the stains with a cloth soaked in bleach. Leave for 1 hour, then wash off.

+ To remove **tea or coffee stains** from laminate, make a thin paste of bicarbonate of soda and water, cover the stain and leave for a couple of hours. Wipe clean with a damp cloth.

COOKTOP

+ **Clean** the outside of the oven and around the hot plates with a damp cloth dipped in bicarbonate of soda.

+ To remove **stains** on the cooktop, dissolve 1 teaspoon bicarbonate of soda in 1 cup boiling water until it fizzes, then pour over the stains. Leave it for 5 minutes, then wipe off.

+ For **burnt-on food**, make a sloppy paste of bicarbonate of soda, coarse salt and white vinegar and leave overnight.

+ **Greasy tiles** around the cooktop can be wiped with white vinegar.

DISHWASHER

+ Cloudy or **dull glassware** will come out of your dishwasher crystal clear and sparkling if you add 1 tablespoon Epsom salts to the wash.

+ **Built-up stains** inside a dishwasher can be removed by adding 1 cup white vinegar in the soap dispenser, or simply in the washer, and washing on the normal cycle. It never fails to clean.

+ Save time **unpacking** the dishwasher by loading all the knives together, all the spoons together and all the forks together.

Dishwasher tablets

+

Instead of using commercial dishwashing detergent tablets and rinse aid in your dishwasher, use bicarbonate of soda instead of the detergent and white vinegar instead of rinse aid. They do just as good a job, if not better.

FREEZER

+ Write a list of your **chest freezer contents** on the freezer door and update it when putting food away or taking food out. It saves items 'getting lost', and you'll always know what you have in stock.

+ Freeze **tomatoes** by cutting them into thick slices, freezing between sheets of baking paper, then lifting into storage containers.

+ To **peel tomatoes** simply, wash them, seal in bags and freeze. While they are thawing, you will find the skins peel off easily.

+ If you buy large quantities of **bacon**, cut off the rinds, roll up each slice, put the rolls side by side in a shallow container, cover and freeze. The individual rolls of bacon can then be easily removed and thawed for use without defrosting the whole batch.

+ If you have a **passion fruit** vine that gives you too much fruit to eat immediately, cut them in half, scrape the pulp into ice-cube trays and freeze. They make delicious ice blocks and are very refreshing served in a glass of lemonade. Use them as a topping for ice cream or pavlova, or mix them with icing sugar to make an icing for cup cakes.

+ Always pick **herbs** at their best moment. If you don't need to use them straightaway, chop and pack into ice-cube trays, top up with water and freeze. When frozen, you can tip out and store the herb cubes in a freezer container or bag. The herb cubes can be added to sauces, casseroles or soups.

+ For school or **packed lunches** in hot weather, prepare sandwiches the night before and freeze. The next morning they will keep fresh and cool as they defrost. Frozen juice boxes make great coolers in a lunch box. Even wrapped chocolate bars can be frozen.

+ When **lemons** are plentiful, wash and slice them, and put in the freezer on a tray. When frozen, bag the slices and they'll be ready for using in drinks.

+ Freeze the empty peels of squeezed lemon halves and they can be easily grated for **flavouring cakes** and biscuits.

+ Freeze **lemon juice** in ice-cube trays. Tip out the cubes into a container and keep in the freezer to use in drinks or cooking.

+ Keep a tray of uncooked biscuits in the freezer – that way you can always pop them in the oven if **unexpected guests** arrive.

+ Instead of spending time **rubbing butter into flour** for pastry or scones, take the butter straight from the freezer and grate it. Then it only takes half a minute to stir in.

+ No room in your freezer for a full loaf of **bread**? Save empty bread bags and unpack the bread into several smaller packages. They'll fit in convenient spaces and defrost quickly when you need them.

+ A supply of fresh **breadcrumbs** on hand is a great time saver. Buy day-old bread (it's usually reduced in price late in the day) mix to crumbs in a food processor and freeze in a large container you can add to. When required for crumb coatings, you can take out a small amount and return the rest to the freezer.

+ An easy way to **make breadcrumbs** is to take a slice of bread straight from the freezer and grate it on the coarse side of a grater.

+ When **baking pies** for the freezer, decorate the top of the pie with the first letter of the contents – it saves on labelling.

+ To prepare uncooked **meat patties** for freezing, spoon the meat into paper muffin cases, place on top of one another and then squash. The patties will separate easily while still frozen.

+ Use spring clothes pegs to close **half-used bags** of frozen vegetables, so they don't spill in the freezer.

+ Re-use the insert trays from boxes of chocolates as **ice-cube trays**.

+ Use jelly instead of fruit juice to make **ice blocks** at home. Make a packet of jelly as directed, pour into ice block moulds and freeze. You'll find they don't drip like regular ice blocks.

+ To thaw **frozen fish**, cover it with cold milk and leave until soft. The milk gives the fish a fresh flavour and could make the base of a sauce, with chopped dill or parsley, white pepper and grated Cheddar.

+ To ensure open packs of **grated cheese** don't go mouldy, keep in the freezer rather than the fridge. When needed, take out the required amount and return the pack to the freezer. No need to defrost.

+ Store home-made **meatballs** in egg cartons. Lay a sheet of cling wrap over the open carton, pop a meatball into each section, fold in the ends and the sides of the cling wrap, then place the whole carton in the freezer. The meatballs will stay fresh and stay in shape.

+ Keep an oven mitt near your chest freezer to avoid getting **ice burns** when you take food out.

+ Use a solution of 2 tablespoons salt and 2 tablespoons bicarbonate of soda in a pan of hot water to rinse out the **freezer compartment**. It cleans effectively and the cloth won't stick.

KETTLES AND JUGS

+ A **decanter or carafe** can be cleaned by half-filling with warm, soapy water and adding 2 tablespoons uncooked rice. Leave for 30 minutes, swirling the rice around occasionally, and then pour the water away. Rinse well and leave to drain.

+ Coarse sand is excellent for cleaning **stained glass vases** and jars. Fill with soapy water and add a small amount of sand. Leave to stand for a while, shaking gently now and then.

+ To clean glass and china **teapots**, add 2 teaspoons bicarbonate of soda, fill with hot water and leave to soak overnight. In the morning simply empty and rinse.

+ To keep **vacuum flasks** fresh, wash and dry thoroughly then add 1 teaspoon bicarbonate of soda and replace the lid. Remember to wash out the flask before your next use. After rinsing your vacuum flask, you can add a few drops of vanilla essence if you like – it will stop the flask smelling mouldy and add a nice taste to your coffee.

+ To clean inside an **electric kettle**, fill it with water and add a few slices of lemon. Bring to the boil and leave for a couple of hours before rinsing thoroughly.

+ If you live in a **hard water** area and find your kettle gets furred up, cover the element with water, add 2 tablespoons malt vinegar and leave overnight. Rinse well and the inside will look clean as new.

MICROWAVE

+ Does your microwave get splattered with food regularly because you forget to use the special **microwave covers**? Store the covers in the microwave: that way it's impossible for anyone to forget and you don't need to go looking for them either.

+ To **clean** your microwave quickly and remove any lingering odours, squeeze a few drops of lemon juice or diluted lemon essence onto a clean, damp cloth. Heat the cloth in the microwave for 20 seconds only. Cool slightly before using it to wipe the microwave clean.

+ When cleaning **baked-on food** from your microwave, first put a cup of soapy water inside and allow to boil. The steam will loosen any stubborn food so that it's easily wiped off.

OVEN

+ Check your **oven handbook** for any special instructions. Unless it advises otherwise, you can clean your oven immediately after use with a cloth wrung out well in hot water and washing soda. Leave the door ajar for a time. If the door is left ajar in the last stages of cooling, it avoids condensation.

+ For an environmentally friendly cleaner for **burnt-on grease**, mix sufficient bicarbonate of soda and water to form a stiff paste and spread it over the inside of the oven, then heat for 30 minutes on a low setting. When the oven has cooled, brush the soda off – it will remove all traces of burnt fat and grease.

+ To loosen **stubborn foods** that have been baked on, place 4 table-spoons bicarbonate of soda in the bottom of a non-metallic baking dish and add just enough water to cover the bottom of the dish. Heat the oven on low heat for 30 minutes, switch off and leave the dish in the oven overnight. Wipe over in the morning.

+ **Clean** an oven with 3 tablespoons Napisan mixed with 500ml water. Pour over the bottom of the oven (switched off) and, 2 hours later, scrape off the grime. Also use for oven walls. The oven will be sparkling clean and won't smell when turned on.

+ For **very dirty ovens**: heat the oven to warm and then switch off. Place 1 cup cloudy ammonia and 1 cup hot water into an old baking dish and place in the warm oven for 30 minutes. Then wipe off the burnt-on grime with a damp scourer dipped in bicarbonate of soda, and finish off with a sponge dipped in white vinegar.

+ Soak heavily soiled **oven racks** overnight in the sink. Dissolve ½ cup bicarbonate of soda in enough hot water to cover the racks. In the morning, most of the baked-on grease will wipe off easily. Repeat for really stubborn grime.

+ If your oven cleaner leaves an **unpleasant smell** in the oven when you turn it on, place 2 pieces of orange peel on an oven tray and bake for a few minutes. The bad odour will simply disappear.

+ **Glass oven doors** can be cleaned quite simply. When the oven is cold, just soak a couple of kitchen towels in ordinary malt vinegar. Leave the paper stuck to the glass for about 15 minutes, then wipe the doors. The solution will even take off stubborn deposits. Clean glass doors regularly with a solution of washing soda and water.

+ To remove the **stale smell** of cooked food, put the grated zest of ½ orange and ½ lemon in an ovenproof dish. Place in a low oven until quite dry.

POTS AND PANS

+ To clean **rust** from pots and pans, use a bit of tomato paste and lemon juice. Gently scrub with a scourer and see the difference the acid makes. They'll look as good as new.

+ Harsh **scourers** and abrasives scratch and wear the surface of aluminium, exposing the underneath surface. It is better to leave saucepans slightly discoloured, but with their protective coating.

+ To clean a **burnt saucepan**, fill with cold water and add 2 teaspoons bicarbonate of soda. Boil for a few minutes, cool and then scrub the pan. You may have to repeat this a few times.

+ To clean a **badly burnt** saucepan, sprinkle household salt over the bottom and cover with vinegar. Leave for 2 hours, then rub with a nylon scourer and rinse clean.

+ To remove grease stains from **electric frying pans**, dip steel wool in methylated spirits and rub stains lightly. Finish with bicarbonate of soda for shine.

+ Keep **iron cookware**, such as a wok, free from rust by coating lightly with oil after you've washed and dried it.

+ Extend the life of a **pressure cooker** sealing ring by running cold water inside the lid immediately after use so as to harden the seal.

+ No lid for your **casserole dish**? Cover with foil, then crinkle around the edge to fit securely

+ Lengthen the life of your **double boiler** by putting marbles in the bottom with the water. Then, when the water is almost gone, you'll hear the marbles rattling around, rather than letting it boil dry.

SINK

+ Try this instant reviver for a **dull stainless steel** sink or any fittings: simply put a small amount of baby oil on a soft cloth and rub over the surface gently for a beautiful shine.

+ If the **plug** for the kitchen sink, or any other sink for that matter, gets in the way, put a self-adhesive cup hook on the wall near where the plug is needed. Now you can hang it out of the way when not in use.

+ Use double-sided tape to attach a clothes peg to the wall near the sink – it makes an ideal hanger to store and dry out **rubber gloves**.

+ Clean a **sink grate** by scrubbing with steel wool.

+ Until you have time to change the washer on a **dripping tap**, tie a piece of string around the rim of the tap, just long enough to reach the drain. Drops will slide silently down the string and stop the dripping noise driving you mad.

+ Use mint to freshen a **garbage disposal unit** in a sink. Simply feed through a few sprigs every now and then. This will also freshen the drainage pipes and give off a pleasant smell.

+ Grease is the most common cause of a **blocked sink**. The grease sets firm as it flows down the cold pipe away from the hot sink. One solution is to make a hole in the fat by pushing a piece of flexible wire down the pipe. Keep working it until you make a good-sized hole, then pour boiling water down the hole. Continue both steps until the blockage is removed.

+ If the hot water treatment fails to clear a blocked sink, use a **sink plunger** placed over the sinkhole and pump very vigorously.

+ If you don't have a plunger, place the neck of an **empty plastic bottle** in the plughole and very quickly squeeze it a few times. Hey presto, the sink will be cleared.

+ If this fails, for **metal pipes** only, make a solution of 125g caustic soda to 5.75 litres water by slowly adding the soda flakes to the warm water, stirring until dissolved. Pour down the sink.

+ If this fails, place a bowl or bucket under the U-bend under the sink, release the nut, then **manually clear** the blockage in the bend. Using a commercial drain cleaner regularly, as directed, should prevent further problems.

Drain cleaner

+

Pour 1 cup washing soda, or ½ cup bicarbonate of soda, down the drain followed by ½ cup white vinegar. Apply a plunger and briskly work up and down. Then pour boiling water down the drain until the blockage is cleared.

STORAGE

+ Grind **coffee beans** yourself, just before you use them, to retain maximum flavour.

+ Store whole or ground **coffee beans** in an airtight container in the fridge or freezer to maintain their flavour.

+ When refilling your flour, rice and other **containers**, cut the 'best before' date from the packet and attach it to the container with sticky tape.

+ Before adding fresh **eggs** to another batch, make a cross on the older eggs with a whiteboard marker to make sure they're used first.

+ Store small bottles of **essences** in a round container, large enough to hold all the bottles you have. It keeps them neat and upright and can be turned around easily to select the one you need.

+ Store **popping corn** in a jar in the fridge. Add a little water to keep it moist and you will find more kernels 'pop' when they are cooked.

+ Store jars of **peanut butter** upside down so that the excess oil will be at the bottom when you turn it over to use.

+ To freshen **peanuts**, place them in the microwave for 1 minute and then allow to cool.

+ Shelling a quantity of **walnuts** can be hard work but, if you soak them in water overnight, they will open easily. Also, the kernels will plump up and come out in perfect halves.

+ Instead of pouring **cooking oil** from a large heavy can or bottle, fill a plastic sauce bottle with oil. Keep it handy for small squirts into the frying pan.

+ You can make useful **funnels** of different sizes by cutting plastic bottles some distance down from the neck. For a funnel for small amounts of dry ingredients use the corner of an envelope with the tip cut off.

FOOD

BAKING

+ If a recipe calls for a **ring tin** and you don't own one, use an ordinary cake tin or casserole dish with an empty washed tin in the centre. Fill the central tin with baking weights or uncooked rice or beans. Grease the cake tin and the central tin very well.

+ When making a **fruit cake**, cut a piece of thin cardboard, or two layers of brown paper and a layer of baking paper and grease both well. Fit into the tin, pour in the mixture and cook the cake at a low temperature. A lovely thin brown crust will form on the bottom and the cake will not burn.

+ If you need an extra large piece of **waxed paper**, seal several smaller pieces together with a hot iron. The join cools in a few minutes.

+ To make a **dusting powder** for cake tins, which prevents sticking and gives a crisp finish to cakes, combine 2 tablespoons plain flour and 1 tablespoon caster sugar. Mix well and keep in an airtight jar.

+ To **grease cake tins**, use a mixture of 2 teaspoons vegetable shortening to 1 teaspoon flour.

+ Rock-hard **butter** from the fridge will cream more easily if you simply grate it first.

+ To **test** if a cake is cooked, lightly press the centre with your fingertips. The cake should spring back immediately and give only lightly to pressure. You could also insert a long skewer into the centre of the cake. If any mixture sticks to the skewer, the cake needs longer.

+ A food processor will turn ordinary sugar to **caster sugar** if you find yourself without.

+ If a butter or fruit cake appears a little **overcooked** and dry when you take it out of the oven, place a thick folded towel over the top of the cake as it cools. This will soften the texture considerably.

+ You can double the volume of your **butter** by whipping up 500g butter until soft and fluffy, then slowly adding ½ cup cold water, ½ cup olive oil and a pinch salt. Beat until completely mixed. Store in the fridge and it will remain soft even at cold temperatures.

+ If your **brown sugar** has turned hard, put it in a bowl and cover with a damp cloth for a few hours (or overnight) and it will be softened and ready to use.

+ **Sticky ingredients** such as honey and treacle will run off a spoon if it is dipped in hot water first. If measuring it in a cup, grease the inside or dust well with flour.

+ A few drops of glycerine added to **egg whites** while you are beating will make them firm.

+ When frothing an **egg white**, add 1 teaspoon cream of tartar and 2 teaspoons cold water. This makes the egg white froth quickly and increases the quantity too.

+ Make **buttermilk** or sour cream by adding ½ teaspoon lemon juice to 1 cup of milk or cream.

+ To prevent the top of a cake **cracking**, lightly brush it with water before baking. Bad cracking means your oven was too hot.

+ **Nuts** can be ground easily in a food processor, or put them into a plastic bag and crush with a rolling pin.

+ To cook **pikelets** with an even, pale brown surface, rub the frying pan with a cut potato for each batch, instead of greasing. Drop the mixture from the tip of a spoon for a good shape.

+ A removable **ice-block divider** from an ice-cube tray is great for cutting biscuit dough evenly.

+ Christmas **mincemeat** is delicious in rock buns. Add about 2 tablespoons to the mixture to give them a spicy flavour.

+ When you're making **oatmeal** biscuits, toast the oats briefly in the oven first to enhance the flavour.

+ For **light pastry**, replace half the quantity of water with lemon juice.

+ When making **sweet pastry**, add 1 tablespoon custard powder and roll out the finished pastry in custard powder. This improves both the texture and taste. For a change of flavour, replace 1 tablespoon flour with 1 tablespoon custard powder in your favourite biscuit recipe.

+ Try rolling rich **flan pastry** between 2 sheets of baking paper. There's no mess because you don't need flour and you can lift up the pastry without breaking it.

+ Mix ¼ cup finely chopped unsalted peanuts into your **apple pie** pastry to add a delicious crunchy texture.

+ For a lovely flavour when making a **fruit pie**, grate lemon rind over the base of the pastry shell before adding the fruit filling.

+ If the juice from an **apple pie** runs over in the oven during cooking, shake salt on it. This causes the juice to be burnt to a crisp, so that it can be easily removed.

+ When making **apple pie**, sprinkle 2 tablespoons rolled oats over the apples in the filling to absorb the excess liquid during cooking. Or sprinkle a little semolina (or wheat flake cereal) over the pastry base before adding the filling. You won't be able to taste the semolina and your pie will have a lovely firm base. Or sprinkle the base with a little rice flour before adding the fruit. It absorbs the juice and stops the pastry getting soggy.

+ **Apple pie** made with raw apples will be lighter if the sugar is sprinkled on all layers of fruit except the top one, as sugar against the pastry turns it soggy.

RECIPE

Royal Melbourne scones

+

4 cups self-raising flour, sifted
1 good pinch of salt
300ml milk
300ml cream

+

Mix all the ingredients together and gently knead.
Cut with a scone cutter – don't twist the cutter or you
will get 'leaning tower of Pisa' scones. Place on
a lined baking tray and bake in a hot oven
for 12 minutes or until well risen and hollow
sounding when tapped on the bottom.

+ An **apple slice** will be lighter if the slice layer is partially cooked before spreading with the stewed apples.

+ When you cook **scones**, try replacing 2 tablespoons of the milk with natural yoghurt. This makes the scones much lighter and gives them a delicious flavour, too.

+ For **lighter scones** add 1 tablespoon cornflour for each 1 cup of flour.

+ Leave the oven door ajar when cooking **meringues**.

+ An easy way to melt **chocolate** for cooking is to make a cup out of aluminium foil, butter it slightly, put squares of chocolate in it, then put the cup into the oven while it is preheating. The chocolate will slide easily out of the foil.

+ To liven up a simple **madeira cake**, sprinkle the top with 1 grated apple mixed with 2 teaspoons caster sugar and ½ teaspoon cinnamon before baking.

+ Equal parts of raw sugar and coconut sprinkled on a plain **butter cake** before baking makes a quick and easy topping.

+ If dates are included in your **fruit cake** recipe, sprinkle with lemon or kumquat juice and leave to stand for 1 hour.

+ Boil any dried fruit for 5 minutes to let it swell and then cool down before mixing for a **fruit cake**. It will be deliciously moist.

+ Place a container of water in the bottom of the oven when cooking rich **fruit cakes**. The steam creates a deliciously moist cake.

+ To stop raisins and sultanas from sinking to the bottom of a sultana cake or your **Christmas cakes**, simply toss them in flour before stirring gently into the mixture.

+ Instead of adding brandy to a **fruit cake** mixture, when you get the cake out of the oven, poke a few holes in the top and sprinkle the amount of brandy over the cake. Leave in the tin until quite cold.

+ Before putting a **strudel topping** on a cake, brush the surface with milk – the topping will stay in place better when the cake is cut.

+ For a more moist **chocolate cake**, dissolve the cocoa in the milk instead of mixing it with the dry ingredients.

+ When making a **sponge**, heat the sugar in a covered dish in the preheating oven, while you are weighing out other ingredients, then tip it on the eggs. This halves the beating time and makes a lighter sponge.

+ To **slice a sponge** in half easily, place a strong cotton thread around it, cross over in front, pull through and – voila – two perfect layers!

+ Use the curved edge of a grapefruit knife for cutting out the centre of **cup cakes** to make butterfly cakes. It removes the dome of the cake very neatly without causing crumbling.

+ Make a **packet cake** extra moist and flavoursome by adding ½ cup sour cream to the mixture.

+ Add a beaten egg white to **lamington** icing. If you refrigerate the cake before icing, it makes the job easier. If you apply the icing and coconut to semi-thawed frozen cake it won't sink in and make the lamingtons soggy.

+ For a special occasion, deluxe finish, put a marshmallow topping on a **chocolate cake** as a change from icing.

+ **Icing** will stick better to the top of a fruit cake if it has been brushed with apricot jam thinned with brandy.

+ If **icing sugar** becomes lumpy in the packet, place it in a plastic bag and roll it with a rolling pin. If icing sugar has become hard and dry, put it in the oven for a few minutes and it will soften. (If you buy 'icing sugar mixture' it has additives to prevent it clumping and becoming hard.)

+ Keep a new eye dropper in your baking drawer. If **icing** needs to be delicately coloured, use the eye dropper to add the colour drop by drop.

+ A teaspoon of custard powder added to the icing sugar and a few drops of almond or vanilla essence makes a good pale **yellow icing**.

+ Butter icing mixed with **kumquat juice** gives a fruity tang to the icing for fruit and plain cakes.

+ If you are making icing for a cake but add too much water, and then have no icing sugar left, try adding **custard powder**. It works just as well and has a delicious taste.

+ Use a single cup tea diffuser to **dust icing sugar** onto cakes. It's easy to dispense and the unused sugar can be returned to the packet.

+ When **icing the top of a cake** only, wrap foil or greaseproof paper around the cake to prevent the icing dripping down the side.

+ Dress up plain cakes and make them extra special with **chocolate lace**. Draw the shape you want on a sheet of baking paper. Pipe the melted chocolate around the outside of the shape, then fill in with lacy lines. Leave to set at room temperature. If making the lace in hot weather, refrigerate it for a few minutes so that the chocolate will set.

+ **Whipped cream** stays fresh for several days if a pinch of bicarbonate of soda is added during the whipping.

+ If **cream** must be whipped several hours before it is needed, add honey instead of sugar to keep it firm.

+ Fresh cream will not ooze out of cakes if a little **gelatine** is dissolved with warm water and added to the cream. Leave until it is just setting before filling the cakes.

+ If cream you are whipping suddenly **turns to butter**, don't despair. Pour off the buttermilk and continue beating, adding the buttermilk back in gradually. A few drops of vanilla improves the flavour.

+ **Cream for sponges** will stay fresh and firm if 1 teaspoon brandy is added during the whipping.

+ **Evaporated milk** can be whipped to taste like cream if it is chilled for 24 hours first and 1 tablespoon icing sugar added for each tinful.

+ For professional looking **lettering** on an iced cake, trace your message onto greaseproof paper first, place it on the cake, then prick through it with a pin to mark the icing. It works every time.

+ An egg slicer will cut uniform slices of **banana** for decorating cakes.

+ To keep a neat, crumb-free surface on a **novelty cake**, cook it the day before you decorate it. After cooking, keep the cake in an airtight container in the fridge overnight and decorate the cake when cold. Coat the cake with a thin layer of icing or frosting first to 'seal' the crumbs on the cake. Don't return the spatula coated with crumbs to the clean icing bowl. Finish with the remaining icing.

+ If you regularly bake cakes for **fetes and fairs**, but find transporting them difficult, look out for pretty plates at second-hand shops. They cost very little, make a nice rigid base, and can be sold with the cake for the customer's convenience.

+ A salt shaker filled with **hundreds and thousands** makes it easier to decorate cakes neatly and evenly without waste.

+ When **transporting** an iced cake, stick toothpicks around the edge of the cake to a depth of 1cm. Cover the cake with cling wrap, allowing the wrap to stand on the toothpicks. This stops the wrap from clinging to the icing and pulling it away.

+ Marshmallows make great **candle-holders** on birthday cakes – they prevent wax running onto the cake.

+ Soft **stale biscuits**, not iced or cream-filled, can be restored quickly to their former crispness. Spread them out on a baking tray and heat in a 140°C oven for 10 minutes.

+ To keep **biscuits crisp**, add a few grains of uncooked rice to your biscuit tin.

+ A good sound apple will keep a **fruit cake** moist if it is kept in the cake tin after the cake has been cut.

+ When **storing** a large cake in a tin, you will find it easier to get the cake in the tin if you place the cake on the inside of the lid and then put the bottom of the tin over the top. It also makes it easier to remove the cake later.

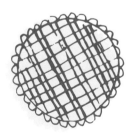

Cake tins

✦

When cutting baking paper, lay 4–6 sheets on top of each other, then cut out. That way you'll have several ready for the next baking day and you can keep them in the baking tin in the cupboard.

✦

To make a special sized cake tin, press a double layer of foil around the inside or outside of a saucepan or casserole dish to achieve the shape you want. Then carefully remove the foil and place it on a baking tray to fill.

✦

When preparing a cake tin, fasten the lining paper to the tin with clothes pegs. This will stop the paper moving while it's being greased.

✦

Use a permanent marker to write the size on the bottom of your cake and slice tins. This will save you time measuring the tins each time they are called for in a recipe.

✦

Clay flowerpots are wonderful for baking bread and cakes – they retain heat in the same way as the old brick bakers' ovens. Just remember to put foil over the drainage hole in the bottom of the pot.

BARBECUES AND BURGERS

+ Brush **oil or marinade** onto barbecued or grilled meat with a 'switch' you make from a selection of fresh herbs tied into a bunch. This gives a delicious, delicate herby flavour.

+ Brush **lemon juice** over meat, in particular veal or lamb chops, to tenderise it while adding flavour.

+ For **tender steak**, rub it with a mixture of half lemon juice and half Worcestershire sauce. Leave it in this mixture for 30 minutes before cooking.

+ Leftover juice from canned peaches, pineapple or apricots can be used as a delicious **baste** when cooking pork or chicken. Keep it refrigerated until needed.

+ If you are barbecuing a lot of **sausages**, thread them onto long skewers first: you'll find them much easier to turn.

+ To prevent **rissoles** cracking apart, simply dip them in water before you roll them in flour.

+ Grated **cheese or peas** give great flavours when making rissoles.

+ Save the **wooden sticks from ice blocks**; wash, dry and store them for when children are coming to a barbecue. Push barbecued rissoles or meatballs onto the sticks for children to hold.

+ Cook your **hamburgers faster** by making a small hole in the middle of the patty, like a doughnut. As the burger cooks, it will swell up and fill the hole.

+ Roll out rissole mixture on a sheet of greaseproof paper and cut into shapes with a **scone cutter**.

+ When **shaping rissoles**, keep your hands wet to prevent sticking.

+ To avoid messy fingers, use a **metal ice cream scoop** to make rissoles or burgers. Press the mixture into the scoop with an egg slice, then turn out the rissoles onto the hotplate and flatten with the egg slide. Perfect rissoles every time!

+ If you are feeding friends who dislike onions in their rissoles or burgers, make them a **different shape** to those that have onion added, so they are instantly recognisable.

+ When making **burgers for small eaters**, cut the bun into thirds rather than halves. Remove the middle third of the bread, or use it to give an extra layer in an adult's large burger.

+ A tasty variation for **hot dogs** is to add mashed potato to the bread rolls with the frankfurter and sauce or mustard, and then crisp them in a hot oven. Great in winter.

BREAD

+ If you can't find a warm place to leave your **yeast dough** to rise, sit the covered bowl on top of a hot water bottle. You'll probably have to change the water only once, and the dough rises beautifully. Or leave it in the car in the sun.

+ To keep a **bread bin** fresh, wipe with a cloth dampened with white vinegar, then sprinkle 1 teaspoon bicarbonate of soda in the bottom and cover with greaseproof paper. Don't let dry crumbs accumulate in the bin.

+ For **garlic bread** with a difference, spread garlic butter onto the bread, top with grated cheese and a small amount of grated onion. Cook in a moderate oven for 10 minutes and serve while still hot.

+ When making **herb bread**, mix a little mustard with the herb butter before spreading on the bread.

+ When buttering **crackers**, place them on a slice of bread and they won't break as easily.

+ To make perfect **fairy bread**, cut the crusts off slices of bread, then butter them evenly. Pour hundreds and thousands onto a plate and the press bread, butter-side down, onto the plate. Try chocolate hazelnut spread instead of butter occasionally – it makes the hundreds and thousands stick better and children love the taste.

+ To freshen **stale bread**, sprinkle the loaf with water and heat in a moderate oven for 10 minutes, or sprinkle with a little water and wrap in aluminium foil before putting in the oven.

Yeast starter

+

To make a yeast starter for bread, take 1 potato,
1 tablespoon hops, 1 tablespoon sugar, 1 tablespoon
plain flour and 2 raisins. Wash and quarter the potato
but do not peel it. Boil the potato in a saucepan with
the hops until soft, then drain off the water and keep
it. Mash the potato and hops with the sugar and flour.
Mix with the potato cooking water and place in
a glass jar with the raisins. Seal tightly and leave
in a warm place to ferment. When baking,
keep back some of the liquid yeast
to start the next culture.

CASSEROLES, STEWS AND PIE FILLINGS

+ Cut meat for stews and casseroles when it is still **slightly frozen**. It is easier to cut, so you can get evenly sized cubes.

+ To **coat meat cubes** with flour, place the meat in a bag with salt, pepper and flour and shake well.

+ When **coating meat with flour** for casseroles, add some mustard powder for a real tang.

+ If you have **over-salted** a stew or casserole, add 1 whole peeled potato or 1 teaspoon soft brown sugar to correct the flavour.

+ To **thicken** stews, casseroles or savoury pie fillings, add mashed potato mix instead of flour. It doesn't go lumpy and tastes better too.

+ If you're making **dumplings** for a winter casserole, add finely chopped fresh parsley and chives and grated cheese into your dumpling mixture for extra flavour.

CHEESE

+ When **storing** cheese in an airtight container in the fridge, place a sheet of kitchen towel in the bottom of the container. It will absorb any moisture and will keep your cheese nice and fresh.

+ If a block of cheese has been left open and gone **dry**, finely grate it and moisten with a little cream. Beat well, add mustard to taste, and you will have a delicious cream cheese spread for biscuits and savouries.

+ When cooking with cheese, always use low to moderate **temperatures** for short periods – high heat or long cooking makes cheese tough and stringy. If adding cheese to a sauce, remove the pan from the heat first; the heat from the sauce will be enough to melt the cheese.

+ To store **cottage cheese** after opening, put the lid back on, turn the container upside down and store in the fridge. The air will be expelled and the cottage cheese will stay fresher for much longer.

DESSERTS

+ When you're making **bread and butter pudding**, use a buttered fruit loaf instead of plain bread and fruit. It's cheaper, much quicker and just as delicious.

+ Roll **shortcrust pastry** between sheets of greaseproof paper and it can be tipped onto pie plates without breaking.

+ To ensure your **pavlova** sets firmly, add a pinch of cream of tartar to the sugar before adding to the egg whites.

+ When making a **pavlova or meringues**, save a little of the mixture, place in a piping bag with a small, plain tube and pipe small designs onto baking paper. Cook in a very low oven – 120°C for 25 minutes or until crisp – and you can use them to decorate desserts.

+ Improve the flavour of **fruit salad** by adding ½ cup fizzy lemonade. It will also keep the salad fresh for several days.

+ When stewing or **poaching fruit**, always boil the water and sugar to a syrup before adding the fruit to prevent the fruit breaking up.

+ Add 2 tablespoons red jelly crystals instead of sugar when **stewing apples**. It turns the apples an attractive pink and makes delicious, thick syrup.

+ Stew **prunes** in black tea sweetened with brown sugar and serve with whipped cream. It's delicious and has a good dark syrup.

+ **Pineapple rings** can be drained on the handle of a wooden spoon held over a bowl to catch the juice. To add fresh pineapple to jelly, cook it first in its own juice or a little water and sugar or the jelly won't set because of the enzymes.

+ Two or three slices of lemon added to **stewed apples** will improve the flavour.

+ A banana added to **rhubarb** when it is cooking adds flavour and thickens the juice. Add a piece of lemon rind to improve the flavour and you will need less sugar. Adding a few drops of vanilla essence during the stewing will take the tartness out of rhubarb. Rhubarb set in strawberry jelly has a great colour.

+ When **making custard**, put the sugar into the cold milk and stir well, then boil and it will not stick to the pan.

+ If **custard curdles or separates**, quickly remove it from the heat and beat with a rotary beater. Stir several times while cooling to prevent a skin forming on top.

+ To stop a **skin forming** on custard or blancmange, sprinkle the sugar on it while it is hot and stir the sugar into the custard when you are ready to serve.

+ When you've made custard or a sauce, press a sheet of greaseproof paper or plastic wrap on to the surface, as this **stops a skin forming** on top. Pull off immediately before serving and add a little extra liquid if the custard or sauce has thickened on standing.

DRINKS

+ A handful of dried dates, soaked overnight in water, make a delicious addition to a **smoothie**. Drain and blend with a banana, 2 tablespoons yoghurt and 1 cup milk for a nutritious breakfast.

+ If you like **Earl Grey tea**, but find it quite expensive, place some ordinary tea leaves in the tea caddy with the Earl Grey variety. The bergamot flavour of the Earl Grey will permeate the plain tea, giving a distinctive flavour at a reduced cost.

+ Add some chopped fresh mint to canned or bottled apple juice and set aside for an hour or more. Strain and pour over ice cubes for a most **refreshing summer drink**.

+ Cut a washed, unpeeled lemon into slices and put in a jug of iced water to make a refreshing **hot weather drink**.

+ Boil a handful of oatmeal in 2 litres water and add the juice of 2 lemons, with or without sugar to taste. It makes a **cooling and refreshing drink**. Keep in a jug in the fridge where children can reach for it on hot days.

EGGS

+ For a perfect **poached egg**, bring some water to the boil and, with a knife, make a whirlpool. Turn the heat to low, then crack an egg into a cup and tip it into the whirlpool. Cook for 3 minutes.

+ Add a slice of lemon to the water when **boiling eggs** to avoid a dark ring around the saucepan.

+ Prick an eggshell with a needle at the round end and it will not **crack** when being boiled.

+ If you are boiling a **cracked egg**, wrap it in foil, twist the ends and boil for the usual time.

+ To keep the **yolk** in the centre (useful if you're making stuffed eggs), stir eggs occasionally when hard-boiling.

+ **Boiled eggs** will not be tough if cooked gently for 15–20 minutes instead of rapidly for a shorter time. Drop in cold water for a few minutes when cooked.

+ Shells do not peel easily from fresh eggs that are **hard boiled**: the eggs need to be a couple of days old.

+ To peel a **hard-boiled egg**, tap firmly to crack the shell and then roll the egg between your hands. The shell and membrane will come away easily.

+ To **separate** an egg, tap the egg sharply with the back of a knife to break the shell in half neatly. Collect the egg yolk in one half of the shell, then pass the yolk back and forth between the two shell halves, allowing the white to drip into a bowl.

+ If you need egg **yolks only** for a recipe, don't throw away the whites but freeze them in ice-cube trays. Freeze one per cube so you know exactly how many you have next time you need egg whites.

+ If you find yourself **without eggs** when a savoury recipe calls for one, try 1 cup cooked rice and a little mashed potato or pumpkin to help bind the ingredients.

+ If you keep chickens and have so many eggs that you need to store them, they will **keep for months** in coarse salt. Stand them on end in a layer of salt, sprinkle salt between them and completely cover, before starting the next layer. A plastic bucket makes an excellent container for this.

FISH

+ When frying fish, sprinkle a little salt in the pan before cooking and the fish **will not stick**.

+ **Poached** fish will keep firm and whole if you add a little lemon juice to the water.

+ Add 1 teaspoon ground ginger to the flour when **coating fish** to give a piquant flavour.

+ Add grated lemon zest or chopped dill to fish **breadcrumbs or batter** for a lovely flavour.

+ For a **crisp fish batter**, mix with beer instead of milk. Add a pinch of bicarbonate of soda for a lighter batter.

Fish patties

+

When you have leftovers from a potato salad, add a beaten egg and a can of salmon or tuna. Mash and roll into balls. Fry the balls in a little oil and serve.

FRUIT

+ **Lemons** will keep fresh for a long time if stored in water in a screw-top jar. Change the water 3–4 times a week.

+ Heat lemons briefly in the microwave (or a hot oven) or in hot water before squeezing and you will get **more juice** from them.

+ If a recipe calls for **a squeeze of lemon juice**, pierce a lemon with a clean knitting needle and squeeze out the required amount. Then you can put it back in the fridge to reuse.

+ How do you remove **lemon zest** from the grater without ripping your fingers or losing most of it? Put a sheet of baking paper over the fine grater before you use it, then just peel off and you will get all the zest.

+ If a recipe calls for orange or lemon **juice but not the zest**, grate the zest anyway and store. Mixed with a little caster sugar, it adds flavour to cakes and biscuits and can be stored in an airtight jar.

+ To make **garnishes** for parties, buffets or cocktails, peel the rind from an orange, lemon or lime. Cut into thin, 10cm strips, then tie into loose knots. For added colour, tie a few of these ribbons together.

+ When **slicing bananas**, dip the knife in lemon juice between each cut to prevent the banana turning brown.

+ When **cutting watermelon**, slice it thinly and most of the seeds will fall out.

+ To prevent **cut apples** from discolouring, sprinkle with lemon juice.

+ To test if a **rockmelon** is ripe, give it a tap with an open hand. It should sound hollow.

JAMS AND PRESERVES

+ Brush the pan with **cooking oil** before you start your jam-making. It stops the jam from frothing up, makes skimming unnecessary and the pan will be easy to clean.

+ A wooden spoon standing in a preserving pan prevents jam from **boiling over**.

+ When making marmalade that requires **finely sliced citrus fruits**, freeze the fruit for an hour or two beforehand. This will stop it squashing as you slice it and losing all the juice that should flavour the jam. Or use the fine blade of a food processor.

+ If you have citrus fruit for marmalade and no time to shred it, put it through a **mincer** set with the coarsest cutter.

+ Moisten cellophane **jam-jar covers** with vinegar or brush the top of the jam with brandy when it is cold before sealing, to prevent mould. Seal the jars when the jam is either boiling hot or completely cold.

+ Jelly will **strain** better through muslin or a jelly bag if you wet the muslin first.

+ When you are **sealing pickle jars** with wax, put a piece of string across the top of each jar in the hot wax. When the wax has set, the string will act as a handle to lift it when you want to take out small quantities of pickle.

MEAT

+ **Schnitzel** is given a lift and distinctive flavour if coated with crushed cheese biscuits instead of breadcrumbs.

+ For **crispy bacon** without the fat, cook it in the microwave on a piece of kitchen towel.

+ Dip bacon in milk before frying and the **rind will not curl**. Alternatively, snip the rind at intervals, with kitchen scissors, or cut it off completely.

+ Dip **sausages** in flour before adding them to the pan – it will help prevent the skins splitting.

+ Boil **salted meat** with 1 teaspoon vinegar and 1 tablespoon sugar or golden syrup. A few cloves or peppercorns add flavour to corned beef.

POULTRY

+ Before **seasoning** a chicken, rub the inside with brandy and brush a little over the skin. It gives a delicious flavour.

+ If you have a collection of fresh breadcrumbs in the freezer, from stale bread, make it into **stuffing** – you can put it back in the freezer to use when you're doing a roast chicken.

+ If you're cooking roast chicken with **roast potatoes**, peel the potatoes and then remove their centres with an apple corer. Insert a tightly rolled bacon rasher in each potato.

+ When **roasting** a chicken, rest it on slices of hard bread (or the rings for frying eggs) in the tin to prevent the crisp skin sticking to the tin.

+ Whenever you have roast chicken, freeze the carcass until you have about 1 kg bones for making great **stock**. Place in a saucepan, cover with water, add a chopped carrot, celery stick, onion, peppercorns and parsley sprigs. Bring to the boil, simmer, uncovered, for about an hour, then strain. Use the stock as the base of soups and casseroles.

RICE, PASTA AND PIZZA

+ Wait until **rice** is half-cooked, then add the juice of ½ lemon. It gives a delicious flavour for both curries and desserts. If you're cooking white rice, the lemon helps it retain its brightness too.

+ When boiling water for **pasta or rice**, always boil the water in your kettle first, then pour it into the saucepan. It's quicker than heating water on the hot plate and will save your energy bills.

+ When making **pizza**, put a round cake rack on top of the pizza tray or baking tray, then cook the pizza on top of the rack. This gives the pizza a lovely crisp base and the tray will catch any drips.

ROAST DINNERS

+ Always place meat into a **cold oven** and on the bottom shelf. Never cook meat above 180°C because it will shrink if cooked in too hot an oven and the fat will make the oven dirty. There is no need to add any more fat when cooking meat – there will be enough fat in it.

+ To prevent a roast joint from **shrinking**, fill a metal bowl with water and put it in the bottom of the oven during cooking.

+ After removing the cooked joint from a roasting tin, empty a tray of ice cubes into the tin. In no time at all, the fat sticks to the ice cubes, making it easy to remove. You'll be left with virtually fat-free meat juices for **making gravy**.

+ Save the outside leaves of lettuce for **reheating leftover roast meat**. Completely cover the meat with leaves, put a lid on the baking dish and heat in a moderate oven or microwave. You'll be amazed how moist the meat stays.

+ When cooking roast pork or chops, instead of making too much **apple sauce**, cut an apple into quarters, leave unpeeled and cook beside the meat for 10 minutes. Or, with roast pork, core an apple per person, fill the core hole with half a sausage or a roll of bacon and bake it with the meat. (This works with potatoes too.)

+ For quick **apple sauce**, flavour a tin of stewed apple or jar of pureed apple baby food with sherry or port and a little cinnamon.

+ If you haven't time to make **mint sauce**, just add 2 teaspoons finely chopped mint and a dash of vinegar to the gravy for roast lamb.

+ For zing in homemade **mustard**, mix with whisky instead of water.

SALADS

+ To crisp a **limp lettuce**, squeeze lemon juice into cold water and leave to soak for a few minutes.

+ Keep **lettuce fresh and crisp** longer by making an X cut in the stem. Stand the lettuce in water for 10 minutes, then turn it upside down and store in the fridge an airtight container.

+ To keep **salad leaves** from going limp, place a saucer upside down in the bowl before adding the salad. Any moisture will run under the saucer, leaving the salad crisp.

+ **Grate cabbage** next time you make a salad instead of shredding it. It gives it a different flavour and is more digestible.

+ If you like **raw onion** in salad but dislike the strong odour, slice and rinse the onion rings under cold water and then pat dry before using. Alternatively, place the slices in a bowl of iced water and leave for a few minutes before draining.

+ If **tomatoes** have gone soft, place them in a small bowl of cold water with 2 teaspoons salt added and leave overnight. In the morning they will be nice and firm again.

+ Whisk together lemon juice and runny honey as a nice change from heavier oil-based **salad dressings**.

+ Save the **flavoured oil** from jars of olives, feta cheese and sun-dried tomatoes. Whisk with vinegar to make a delicious salad dressing.

+ When cutting up a small **beetroot**, use an egg slicer to prevent it sliding around.

SANDWICHES

+ When making **tomato sandwiches** for picnics and lunchboxes, salt the outside of the bread and they won't go soggy.

+ You can also sit the **sliced tomatoes** on fresh bread to absorb the moisture before putting them into the sandwich.

+ **Soften butter** for spreading with a fork dipped in boiling water.

+ When making a large amount of sandwiches, have a pan of just-boiled water standing by. Use **two knives**, and keep one in the water until the other is sticky with spread, then change them over. A heated knife also makes it easier to cut the bread.

+ For a change of flavour, spread meat or salad sandwiches with **hummus** instead of butter or margarine.

VEGETABLES

+ For easy **baked vegetables**, peel and cut them into pieces, toss in a splash of oil, then turn out into a baking dish lined with baking paper. There's no need to turn them during cooking and no mess left behind in the pan.

+ **Roast potatoes** are deliciously different if, instead of flour, you coat them with your favourite soup-in-a-cup mix. Coat in the soup mix, arrange them on a lightly oiled oven tray and roast until the coating becomes crisp.

+ If you're trying to **cut down on oil** in your cooking, dip a pastry brush in a little oil and brush peeled, chopped potatoes for roasting. They will roast just as well as if you'd used pools of unnecessary fat.

+ **Baked potatoes** will be crisper if they are brushed with oil or melted butter before baking. Remove the soft cooked potato inside and mix with fillings such as chopped fried bacon, sliced fried leek and grated cheese. Stuff back inside and reheat.

+ For perfect **crisp potato chips**, boil the thinly sliced potato for a few minutes, pat dry in a clean tea towel, then fry. Firm pumpkin also makes excellent chips.

+ Use a kitchen scourer to **scrub potatoes**. Plastic mesh bags that fruit are packaged in, rolled up and sewn into a ball, are also useful for scrubbing potatoes.

+ A little milk or lemon juice in the water when **boiling potatoes** makes them whiter.

+ For neat cubes for a **potato salad**, cut the potatoes into cubes, place them in a deep steamer basket and cook gently until done. Drain and leave to cool – they should be in excellent cubes.

+ Always open a tin of whole **asparagus** from the bottom – that way the tips will not break off when you remove the asparagus.

+ To speed up the **ripening of an avocado**, place it in a brown paper bag for a few days with a banana. Store at room temperature, out of direct sunlight.

+ To eliminate **smells** when cooking green vegetables, especially cabbage, cauliflower and sprouts, add one of these ingredients to the boiling water: ½ slice bread; 1 slice lemon; 1 bay leaf; 1 teaspoon rice.

+ If a large **pumpkin** softens before you are ready to cook it, chop it into smaller pieces, scrape away any soft patches and pour boiling water over to scald it. Cool and store in the fridge and it will last for another week.

+ To add some zing to **pumpkin soup**, boil a Granny Smith apple along with the pumpkin, then add a pinch each of curry powder and ground ginger when you puree the pumpkin. It will give it a mildly spicy flavour.

+ If you don't have **bamboo shoots** when a recipe calls for them, you can use the white inner stalk of cauliflower instead. White stems of cabbage, cauliflower, spinach or silverbeet can also be used as a substitute for celery in pickles, chutney or Asian cookery.

+ To keep **cauliflower** white while it cooks, add lemon juice to the water.

+ When you are making the cheese sauce for a **cauliflower cheese**, the flavour is improved by adding a dash of nutmeg, a dash of Dijon mustard, or a little crumbled blue cheese along with the Cheddar.

+ If you have bought a bunch of **asparagus** or are picking it from the garden, store it in a jar of water like a bunch of flowers. It doesn't need to be in the fridge.

+ When preparing **broccoli**, there is often a large piece of stalk left over. Instead of throwing it out, steep it in boiling water for a few seconds then freeze it for later use in soups and stir-fries.

+ Instead of boiling **Brussels sprouts**, remove all the leaves and lightly fry them in butter with a little garlic and some fresh chives, or stir-fry in a wok with soy sauce and lemon juice.

+ When cooking fresh **green peas**, add a few pods to the water to keep them green. Add a little mint and sugar to the cooking water, too, for great flavour.

+ Alternatively, don't waste time **shelling peas**. Drop them, pods and all, into the water and bring to the boil. After a couple of minutes, the shells will come to the top, leaving behind the peas. The flavour is excellent too.

+ Use kitchen scissors to snip **parsley and chives**. Rosemary and thyme are easier to chop with a knife.

+ Rinse **parsley** in hot water if you want it to keep its colour.

+ **Parsley** can be spread on a baking tray and baked in a low oven until brittle. Crush or rub the leaves finely and store in an airtight container.

+ **Parsley** can also be frozen – finely chop and store in a freezer bag.

+ Keep **parsley fresh** for several weeks by covering with cold water and leaving for several hours. Then drain, pat dry and place, stalks downwards, in a screw-top jar in the fridge.

+ If you are **short of parsley** for a recipe, use chopped carrot stalks or celery leaves instead.

+ When **chopping mint**, sprinkle the board with sugar. The leaves stay greener and you will find it easier to chop them finely.

+ Don't throw away **celery leaves** – they can be dried and used to flavour soups and stews. Wash the leaves and pat dry, then place between sheets of kitchen towel and microwave for 2–3 minutes. Or, spread on a baking tray and bake in a low oven until brittle. Crush or rub them finely and store in an airtight container.

+ Top and tail **spring onions** and store them in a screw-top jar in the fridge. The smell won't taint other food and they will keep for ages.

·RECIPE·

Quick, easy toppings for baked potatoes:

+

Grated cheese, sour cream and chopped chives

+

Leftover savoury mince or chow mein

+

Tomato salsa, sour cream and mashed avocado

+

Sour cream mixed with a little packet soup mix (such as French onion or spring vegetable)

+ Chop up **onions** under your range hood. The exhaust fan will suck up the fumes and help prevent tears.

+ Stop the tears from **chopping onions**, especially if you're preparing large quantities for pickles, by peeling and cutting onions in half, putting in a plastic bag in a single layer and putting in the freezer. When they're frozen (which usually takes a few hours, depending on the quantity), chop or slice with a sharp knife. Be careful the knife doesn't slip if the onions are very hard; it is best to thaw them for a short time.

+ Peel **pickling onions** in the fresh air to avoid tears and rub your hands with a sprinkling of mustard before washing them.

+ **Onions are easier to peel** if dipped in very hot water for a while.

+ Make a cloth bag out of an old tea towel and use to **store fruit and vegetables** in the fridge. Because the cloth breathes, the vegetables will stay dry and last much longer.

+ **Carrots and parsnips** will keep fresh in plastic bags in the fridge for weeks if you add a sheet of kitchen towel to the bag. This absorbs moisture and keeps the vegetables dry. Change the paper when it becomes damp.

+ Place a slice of carrot in a **garlic press** on top of the garlic you are crushing. When you squeeze the press, the whole of the garlic clove goes through the press and the carrot remains behind.

+ There's no need to peel and chop **garlic** every time you want to use some. Chop a number of cloves in a food processor and store half in a screw-top jar in the fridge. Mix the other half with softened butter. It will last for about 2 months and you can use it straight from the container for garlic bread or frying.

+ A **shrivelled capsicum** will quickly become crisp and smooth again if you put it in an airtight container of water in the fridge. The capsicum should be cut in half and deseeded before putting it in the water and it will remain firm and fresh for a few days.

+ To fill and **bake tomatoes**, put them in muffin tins and they will be easy to handle and there won't be any spillage.

+ Dip **tomatoes** in flour before frying and they will not be watery.

+ Dust thick slices of **tomato** with flour and curry powder and grill or bake to serve with chicken.

+ Use an egg slicer to slice **button mushrooms**. It gives nice even slices and makes the job much quicker.

HEALTH
AND BEAUTY

HEALTH AND BEAUTY HINTS

+ **Garlic breath** will disappear if you chew on whole cloves, fresh mint or parsley leaves.

+ Use hair conditioner instead of soap when you are **shaving your legs**. It softens the hairs and leaves legs feeling beautifully smooth.

+ Boric acid sprinkled into socks will prevent **foot odour**.

+ Rub lemon juice on your hands to **remove stains**. Rub elbows with a squeezed lemon half to soften and whiten them.

+ If you have **sore eyes**, bathe them in cold black tea.

+ Keep wild **eyebrows** looking neat all day by combing with a dab of hair gel on an old toothbrush.

+ Don't waste the stub of an expensive **lipstick** when it's worn down low: use a cotton bud to get the rest out of the tube. You'll find it gives you a defined lip line, as well as making the lipstick last longer.

+ A sprig of fresh mint inside the pillowcase is refreshing for a person **confined to bed** in hot weather.

+ To **clean dentures**, place in a mixture of half water, half white vinegar overnight. Rinse thoroughly.

+ To make your own **bubble bath**, grate a bar of soap and mix with a little grapeseed oil and rose water.

+ If you **run out of toothpaste**, there is a good substitute that most people will already have in their kitchen. Mix bicarbonate of soda with a little water to make a thick paste – you can add a few drops of peppermint essence for flavour – and it does just as good a job.

Make your own soap

✦

Collect your leftover soap scraps in a clean glass jar with enough water to ensure the soap is always well covered. When you have around 300ml, heat in the microwave for 90 seconds to soften the soap to liquid. Transfer to a pump dispenser, allow to cool and you have your own recycled liquid soap.

✦

Or save your leftover scraps of soap in a clean glass jar with a few drops of glycerine. Steam this in boiling water until the mixture softens. When cool, simply mould into a new bar of soap.

FIRST AID AND HOME REMEDIES

+ **Essential oils** can be inhaled, added to your bath, dabbed on your skin or used in massage oils. Their rich, fragrant perfumes calm, soothe, heal, fight infection, revitalise, relax and stimulate the body. The oils are very concentrated and so only a few drops are necessary.

+ For **muscular pain**, mix 6 drops each of eucalyptus and lavender oil together and massage into the painful area.

+ For **indigestion and nausea**, stir 1 drop of peppermint oil into a glass of warm water with a little honey. When sipped, this acts extremely quickly. This also works well to counteract nausea during pregnancy.

+ Children's frozen icy poles (the ones in clear plastic tubes that you cut the tops off to eat) make great **ice packs** for a swollen or bruised area. Wrap one in a tea towel for a small area, or make a large ice pack with a few of them. Once thawed, they can be returned to the freezer.

+ A little methylated spirits alleviates the **pain of sunburn**. Dab it on with cotton wool.

+ Hold **superficial burns** under cold running water for 10 minutes and apply ice in a cloth.

+ Rub **bee and wasp stings** with a cut onion. The pain goes almost immediately and it works for other insect bites too.

+ To quickly remove an **insect from an ear**, hold a torch close to the ear and the insect will come out towards the light.

+ Suck a sugar lump soaked in white vinegar to stop **hiccoughs**, or pour a small amount of vinegar into a glass and drink it.

+ If you find it difficult to **swallow tablets**, mix them with a good spoonful of mashed banana or jam.

+ To prevent **liquid medicine sticking** to the side of a glass, rinse the glass first in hot water. The medicine will run out easily and you'll have no excuse not to drink the lot!

+ Measurements on **medicine glasses** are often hard to read. Paint over the markings with a thin layer of coloured nail polish.

+ Paint the **labels on medicine bottles** with a coat of clear nail polish to prevent obliteration by stains or tearing when wet.

Pimple treatment

+

To heal a pimple quickly, bruise a fresh marigold petal and press it firmly on the pimple for 2–3 minutes. Repeat the application from time to time until there nothing but a trace of redness left.
If a fresh marigold petal is not available, use a fresh marigold leaf.

Facial exfoliant

+

Mix 1 teaspoon caster sugar and
1 teaspoon runny honey. Gently massage
the mixture onto your face and rinse
off with tepid water. This is also
excellent for rough knees
and elbows.

Hand lotion

+

Grate a bar of soap into
a bowl, add 1 cup boiling
water and beat together well.
Add 125g lanolin and 125g
glycerine and beat until frothy.
Store in jars for up
to a year.

HEADACHES

+ Bathe the back of the **neck and temples** with water as hot as you can bear. This relaxes the muscles that supply blood to the brain.

+ Dampen a face cloth with **white vinegar** and lie down with it over your forehead or closed eyes.

+ Put a couple of drops of **lavender oil** on your fingers and massage into your temples.

+ Put a few drops of **lavender oil** in a bowl of warm water, wring out a cloth in it, and apply to the back of the neck.

NAIL CARE

+ **Brittle nails** usually indicate a dietary deficiency. It is commonly known that calcium is necessary for strong nails but the mineral silica is equally important. Helpful foods containing silica include barley, kelp, garlic, onions, parsley, rice, chives, celery, lettuce and sunflower seeds.

+ To **remove stains** from fingernails, dissolve 2 denture-cleaning tablets in a bowl of tepid water and soak the nails for a few minutes.

FLU, COLDS AND SORE THROATS

+ Drink a cup of hot **herbal tea** every hour or so. Blend equal parts of dried peppermint, elderflower and yarrow and brew in a ceramic pot – 1 teaspoon for each cup and one for the pot. Steep for 5 minutes, strain and sip slowly.

+ Turn the herbal tea into a **hot toddy** by adding lemon juice, honey (for sore throats) and a good dash of whisky.

+ To ease a **sore throat**, make a mixture of 1 teaspoon honey with 1 teaspoon lemon juice.

+ An excellent **gargle** for sore throats and coughs is 1 teaspoon salt dissolved in a glass of hot water. If the throat is very sore, add 1 teaspoon bicarbonate of soda too. Gargle with this every 2 hours.

Cough remedies

+

Sip 1 cup of hot milk with 1 teaspoon glycerine added.

+

Mix together 1 tablespoon honey, 1 tablespoon glycerine and the juice of 1 lemon. Sip a teaspoonful as required.

+ If you have a eucalyptus tree nearby, **crushed gum leaves** steamed in hot water and inhaled are good for colds and to clear the head. If you don't have a tree, buy a bottle of eucalyptus oil for steaming. For stuffy noses, put a few drops of eucalyptus or peppermint oil on your handkerchief.

+ Pour a capful of **tea tree oil** into the shower recess as you step in. It also works well in the bath for children. It makes a great inhalant for stuffy noses and a pleasant smelling antiseptic for the drains at the same time.

+ If the **cough** is caused by a crumb in your throat or 'something going the wrong way' raise your arms alternately and hold them above your head in turn. This raises the diaphragm and relieves pressure. Sipping on hot water will also help.

HAIR

+ If your hair is **coloured**, always test any treatments (even natural treatments) on a small strand first.

+ Natural yoghurt makes a great hair **conditioner**. Leave in the hair for a few minutes, then rinse. This is a great way to make good use of yoghurt that is past its use-by date.

+ Need a beautiful way to use up **flat beer** after a party? Wash and rinse your hair then pour flat beer over your hair, leave for a couple of minutes and rinse out with cold water for a conditioning treatment.

+ For beautifully **shiny hair**, after you've shampooed, massage a mixture of 1 beaten egg and the juice of 1 lemon into your hair. Leave for a while and then rinse out.

+ To **lighten** hair naturally in summer, after shampooing rinse in water softened with the juice of 1 lemon.

+ Add 1 tablespoon white vinegar or a few drops of olive oil to the final rinse to remove all traces of shampoo and make hair **glossy**.

+ Cover your hairbrush with a silk scarf and brush vigorously to bring up a **sheen**.

+ Remove **oily build-up** on combs and brushes by soaking them in 1 litre warm water with 3 tablespoons bicarbonate of soda added. Rinse in clean water.

+ If you **colour** your hair at home, smear petroleum jelly around your hairline and over your ears before applying the colour to prevent tell-tale stains on your skin.

+ If you need to wear **glasses** while colouring your hair, prevent the earpieces from staining by cutting two fingers from a pair of plastic gloves to slip over them.

+ When your hair has been washed and blow-dried and you want to keep it looking 'salon perfect', sleep on a **satin pillow** or pin a silk scarf over your pillow. Your hair will be shiny and easy to brush in the morning.

·RECIPE·

Dry hair treatments

+

Rub warm olive oil or corn oil into your scalp, cover with a towel and leave for 1 hour before rinsing off.

+

Mix 1 teaspoon white vinegar in ½ cup water and massage into the hair weekly. Leave for 3 minutes, then rinse off.

BATHROOM

BATHROOM HINTS

+ To clear a **sink blockage**, sprinkle some bicarbonate of soda down the plughole, then follow it with some white vinegar so that it froths up. Leave for a minute then place the plunger over the plughole with the hot water tap running and suction firmly.

+ Save the plastic caps from 2 litre milk or juice bottles and press onto the bottom of a bar of **soap**. This will help to keep the soap dry by raising it up in the soap dish.

+ If they aren't used often, cans of hairspray and shaving cream can leave **rust marks** on bathroom shelves and surfaces. To prevent this, when you buy a new can, turn it upside down and paint the bottom with a coat of clear nail polish.

+ After **shaving**, rinse the razor and shake it dry, then smear a coat of Vaseline across the blade. This prevents tiny particles of dust (invisible to the naked eye) from blunting the edge of the blade.

+ If you buy a **shampoo** that doesn't agree with your hair, there's no need to waste it. Pour it into a pump action bottle and use it as liquid soap for washing hands.

+ Cut up old **stockings or tights** into small squares and use instead of cotton wool to remove nail polish. When dipped in nail polish remover, it does a better job than cotton wool and doesn't leave behind cotton fibres that can ruin the next coat.

+ To get a great deal more out of **tubes of toiletries** and expensive creams, just cut off the bottom end of the tube bit by bit as you use it. Seal the end with a peg to prevent it drying out. This is a money-saver for all sorts of tubes.

+ Buy a **hat stand** for extra hanging space instead of going to the expense of having wall fixtures installed. Keep it in a corner of the bathroom where the curved arms take up little space. Use it for towels, shower caps and bathrobes. A PVC hat stand is good in the bathroom as it won't be affected by moisture.

MIRROR

+ To stop the bathroom mirror **fogging up**, rub it with a dry bar of soap. Alternatively, rub it with a mix of equal parts glycerine and methylated spirits, or wipe with silicone furniture polish. Polish off with a soft dry cloth.

+ To clean the bathroom mirror, screw up a sheet of newspaper into a ball and then damp with **white vinegar**.

+ **Turpentine** wiped over a mirror will keep it sparkling clean and spot free.

+ Stubborn **stains** on a mirror need a mild borax solution.

+ To remove **hairspray** from bathroom mirrors, wipe with a cloth dabbed in neat methylated spirits.

+ To restore **dull mirrors**, save your tea leaves (just cut open the used teabag if you use them), pour boiling water over the top, leave a while, then strain off the liquid. Use this to dampen and wipe.

BATH

+ If your plughole clogs up and you don't have a plunger, get a **tennis ball** and cut out a section that will fit firmly over the plughole. Push down on it with the palm of your hand 20–30 times. The suction will clear the blockage.

+ Save old nylon stockings and tights to use instead of cloths for **cleaning baths** and wash basins. They will remove dirt without harsh rubbing.

+ To **easily clean low-set baths** without taxing your back, leave a little water in the bottom of the bath and sprinkle cleaner over it. Scrub with a nylon broom.

+ For a **mild abrasive** to clean baths, sinks, toilet bowls and tiles, make a light paste of bicarbonate of soda and water. Shine with white vinegar.

+ **Stains** in the bath can be removed with a paste made of kerosene and bicarbonate of soda, or a paste of borax and lemon juice.

+ Remove **rust stains** in the bath by rubbing with a cloth dipped in white vinegar.

+ To remove unsightly **lime scale** around sink and bath taps, sprinkle with a little white vinegar, leave for a few minutes and rinse off with cold water.

+ If you are going away for an extended time and want to prevent **stains** forming under the taps of porcelain baths and basins, smear Vaseline on the porcelain.

TAPS

+ To remove **rust** from chrome taps, dip a wad of aluminium foil in water and rub vigorously. Rust and other marks will disappear. Chrome can also be polished with methylated spirits.

+ Wipe chrome taps with **silicone furniture polish** – water will then run off and not dry on the chrome.

+ Chrome fixtures will **sparkle** if you spray them lightly with a commercial window cleaner or white vinegar, then polish off with a soft dry cloth.

+ To **clean** chrome fixtures, make a solution of 1 teaspoon powdered water softener and 1 teaspoon washing detergent dissolved in 1 cup warm water. Wipe the marks off the chrome, then rinse and dry with a soft cloth.

+ Polish **stainless steel** sinks and fittings with a soft cloth moistened with kerosene, then a soft dry cloth.

TILES

+ Tiles in the shower recess can be easily and quickly cleaned by wiping with a **steel wool pad** dipped in white vinegar or methylated spirits.

+ **Clean grouting** between tiles with salt on an old toothbrush.

+ To **remove mould** from tiles, use a brush or scourer and scrub with bicarbonate of soda, methylated spirits, cloudy ammonia or Epsom salts.

Bathroom tile cleaner

+

Dissolve 12 drops eucalyptus oil in
2 teaspoons methylated spirits and
add 2 litres tepid water
(this helps dispel the oil).
Keep in a spray bottle and use
to wipe over ceramic tiles.

TOILET

+ If you drop something down the toilet, bend a **wire coat hanger** into a long hook and use it to remove the blockage.

+ To clean the toilet, pour in 1 cup **white vinegar**, leave for a couple of hours and then scrub well. Give the toilet a soapy scrub every couple of weeks and use the vinegar as a regular disinfectant.

+ For badly **stained toilet bowls**, make a thin paste of bicarbonate of soda and white vinegar and scrub well.

+ A few drops of **lemon oil** will make the toilet smell nice.

+ Tablets for cleaning dentures are also great for removing stubborn and unsightly **scale and rust stains** in the toilet bowl. Simply drop 2–3 tablets in the toilet and leave for a few hours. When you flush, the stains should vanish.

+ Alternatively, to remove **rust stains** from the toilet, pour in half a bottle of Coca Cola and leave overnight. In the morning, flush and the rust will all be gone.

SAFETY

+ If you're a bit unsteady, living alone and nervous when taking a bath in case you slip or feel faint, then attach a long cord to the plug and the other end to the bath tap or an object that floats. This will help you **pull out the plug** and drain the water out of the bath quickly if you ever need to.

+ If you find it difficult to pull the plug out of the bath (this can become tricky if you have **arthritic fingers**), put the plug in the toe end of a knee-high stocking. The plug will still fit in the plughole but will no longer be slippery and hard to pull out.

+ Keep a small piece of **shower mat** (15 x 10cm will be enough) with your travel wash bag. You can use it in the shower recess when you're travelling to prevents slips and falls.

SHOWER CURTAINS

+ To clean **plastic shower curtains**, scrub with white vinegar.

+ Every few months, take the curtain down and **wash** it in detergent and bleach. Test the bleach on a hidden piece of curtain first to ensure it won't damage the material.

+ To slow down the **mildew** process on shower curtains, dip a cloth in a solution of supermarket chlorine bleach and rub down the inner side of the curtain every couple of weeks.

+ If a slimy **soap residue** builds up on shower curtains or mats, sprinkle with undiluted liquid bleach, leave for 15 minutes and then rinse off thoroughly with water.

+ If the **rail** for your shower curtain is a little too high, you can add length to your shower curtain by hanging it from two rows of curtain hooks.

LAUNDRY

LAUNDRY HINTS

+ **Treat stains** as soon as they happen (see page 94). The longer they are left, the more firmly they will set in place.

+ Don't be unnecessarily **rough** when washing clothes. Clean by gently squeezing, and rub stains lightly. Don't use over-hot water: cold or lukewarm is quite satisfactory for all but the dirtiest washing.

+ Only ever use '**just enough**' soap powder or laundry liquid. Too much is wasteful and often hinders, rather than helps, cleaning, is bad for the environment and just requires extra rinsing.

+ Keep **woollens** under water as much as possible during washing: lifting them in and out of the water causes unnecessary strain on the fibres.

+ Don't use **bleach** unnecessarily. The best, most efficient, least harmful way to bleach clothes is still by drying them in sunshine and fresh air. Spreading them out on a flat surface and dampening now and again with fresh water will speed up the bleaching process.

+ Lemon juice makes a good **bleach** for white cottons. To bleach, use 1 cup lemon juice in ½ bucket water. A soapy solution with lemon juice added is an effective whitener for cotton fabrics.

+ To keep **colours bright**, add a cupful of white vinegar to your washing machine during the rinse cycle.

+ Before washing **white socks**, soak them in salted water. Stains will then come out easily in the wash.

+ Wash **dark socks** inside nylon stockings to keep them lint free.

+ Wash small **delicate** items inside a pillowcase.

+ When you are **rinsing coloured woollens**, add 1 tablespoon of white vinegar to the final rinse. It keeps the colours bright and is recommended for multi-coloured garments.

+ To find out if a coloured garment is **colourfast** before washing, damp the inside of the hem, then press between two pieces of white cloth with a hot iron. Should any colour come out, you will need to wash the garment separately.

+ When you have to rub the **collar and cuffs** of a shirt with laundry soap, use the tail of the shirt. This ensures even wear.

+ Place freshly laundered items at the bottom of the pile so clothes are used in rotation and receive the same amount of **wear and tear**.

+ Soak **new tea towels** in cold water with a handful of Epsom salts before use to remove the dressing, making them soft and absorbent.

·RECIPE·

Dye fix for corduroy

+

Finely grate 2 potatoes, add ½ cup white vinegar and ¼ cup table salt. Add 4 litres water and leave to stand for 10 minutes. Strain, then let the garment soak in this for 20 minutes before washing. This treatment only has to be done once and the dye should be fixed.

+ Woollen garments that have **shrunk** slightly can sometimes be re-stretched: dissolve 3 tablespoons Epsom salts in boiling water, let it cool, then soak the garment for 30 minutes. Remove, squeeze out the excess water, then stretch into shape. When it is almost dry, press with a cloth between the garment and the iron.

+ When washing **blankets or woollen clothes** to be stored over summer, add a cake of camphor dissolved in hot water to the final rinse. This will discourage moths and silverfish. And 2 tablespoons glycerine added to the rinsing water will keep blankets soft.

+ If a **woollen blanket becomes matted** after washing, dissolve a pack of Epsom salts in hot water and allow to cool. Gently hand-wash the blanket in the cool solution, then leave to soak for 30 minutes. Gently wring out the excess water and dry the blanket in the shade.

+ To wash a **doona or eiderdown**, prepare a large quantity of soapy water (use a wool wash: nothing harsh) and wash by kneading and squeezing. After rinsing thoroughly, wring to remove as much water as possible and carry outside in a laundry basket. Shake vigorously and dry outdoors. Always choose a sunny, windy day to speed up the drying. Continue to shake the doona during and after drying to keep the filling evenly distributed. If necessary, smooth out the cover lightly with a warm iron before it is dry.

+ When you find a mark on your **doona cover** and decide to wash it, put a clothes peg on the mark before taking it off the bed, that way you can easily find and spot clean the cover when it gets to the laundry.

+ Keep scraps of soap in an old stocking and tie both ends – this can be used in the washing machine if you **run out of soap powder**.

+ To get a **starched** look, yet not too stiff, dissolve 3 teaspoons gelatine as directed on the box. Add to 4 litres hot water. Rinse the garments, wring and dry as usual. There will be enough body in the garments to make them look as good as new.

+ Put life back into **net or lace curtains** after laundering. Rehang them, arrange the folds to your liking, then take a can of fabric finish (used to make ironing easier) and lightly spray them – stand about 1 metre away and spray at an angle, so that the spray doesn't penetrate the curtains and dull the windows.

+ **Tie apron strings** when they are washed, to prevent tangling.

+ Soiled **petit point embroidery** can often be freshened by rubbing with bicarbonate of soda. Brush out with a soft brush.

+ **Pollen from lilies** is notoriously difficult to get off clothes. But if you place a piece of Sellotape on top, then peel it off carefully, your garment will be pollen- and stain-free.

+ To keep sheer **terylene curtains** crisp, add a good handful of Epsom salts to the final rinse. Hang them up while still wet (with a towel on the floor to catch any drips) and they will dry uncrushed and crisp.

+ **Slip covers** will have a better fit if stretched back over the furniture while they are still damp.

+ To bleach **delicate lace** that has yellowed with age, soak it in sour milk for several hours and then wash as usual.

STAIN REMOVAL

BALLPOINT PEN
+ Squeeze lemon juice onto the stain, leave for a while, then wash normally. Methylated spirits can also be rubbed into the stain to remove it.

BEETROOT
+ Place a saucer of cold water under the stain and a slice of bread on top. The moistened bread will absorb the stain, then wash the article in the usual way.

BLOOD
+ Soak in cold or tepid water with washing soda added and leave for a while before washing.

+ Or soak in a bowl with a few drops of cloudy ammonia dissolved in 1 litre warm water. Rub with soap and leave for a while before washing.

BLUSHER
+ Dab with methylated spirits, rinse and repeat, adding a few drops of ammonia. Rinse well.

CHEWING GUM
+ Place the garment in the freezer overnight and gum will peel off easily.

+ Soak the article in cold water and then peel the gum off.

+ Rub with an ice cube and then scrape off with a blunt knife.

+ Scrape off as much gum as possible and then rub with eucalyptus oil.

CHOCOLATE, RIBENA AND INK
+ To remove these stains from clothes, carpet and wallpaper, rub with a wet wipe.

COCOA OR CHOCOLATE MILK

+ Soak in cold soapy water, or cover the stain with borax for 2 minutes, then wash in cold water. Pour boiling water through the stained area after washing.

CRAYON ON PAINTWORK

+ Rub with a little toothpaste, leave for a few minutes and then wash off.

CRAYON ON WALLPAPER

+ Rub lightly with dry, soap-filled, steel wool pads

CURRY

Soak in methylated spirits or glycerine before washing as usual. Hang in the sun to dry.

DEODORANT

+ Soak the affected area for 1 hour in a solution of 4 tablespoons white vinegar in 500ml hot water. Then rub with a bar of pure laundry soap.

EGG

+ Sponge with or soak in cold salty water.

EYEBROW PENCIL

+ Apply a grease solvent or dab with a little ammonia on a clean cloth. Rinse in plain water.

FELT-TIP PEN

+ Soak the stain overnight in milk, then launder in the usual way.

FRUIT

+ Immediately rub in salt and then pour boiling water through the stain. Peach, pear and plum stains can also be removed by soaking in cold water first and then in a little hot glycerine; after a while, drop some white vinegar onto the stain, leave for 2–3 minutes and then rinse thoroughly.

GLUE

+ Soak overnight in malt vinegar. Lightly scrub, then machine wash as usual.

GRASS

+ Soak the stains in glycerine or eucalyptus oil for at least 1 hour before washing.

+ Or wet the stain and sprinkle with sugar. Roll up and leave for 1 hour, then wash as usual.

GREASE

+ To remove kitchen grease from T-shirts, wash the shirt in tepid water with borax powder. Then rub the marks with laundry soap. Add a handful of salt to the water to help prevent any colour loss.

+ To remove grease stains from tablecloths, soak overnight in cold water with a large cupful of Napisan, then wash in the usual way the next day.

+ To remove mechanical oil stains, rub with eucalyptus oil, having first put a cloth underneath to catch the grease that comes out of the stain.

+ To clean grease marks from wallpaper, cover the spot with clean white blotting paper and iron with a heated iron. Keep moving clean parts of the blotting paper to the spot until all the grease has been removed.

INK

+ Soak in a solution of citric acid or lemon juice and salt and then wash.

+ Milk will remove ink stains from linen and calico if applied immediately. Soak the affected area in milk for a few minutes, then wash in clean water.

+ Ink can be removed from clothes with a little milk, but it needs to be done as quickly as possible. Soak the inked area in milk for about 20 minutes, then rinse off and dry.

+ To remove black ink from clothing, rinse quickly in cold water. Soak in soapy water with cloudy ammonia added, or make a paste of salt and lemon juice, leave on the stain for a while then wash in soapy water.

+ To remove red ink stains from linen, spread with a paste of mustard powder and water. Leave for 30 minutes or until all the stain is removed.

+ To remove an ink stain from carpet, immediately cover with salt to absorb the stain. Remove the salt by vacuuming or brush off with a stiff broom.

IODINE

+ Iodine stains are easily removed by washing items in warm soapy water with a little kerosene added. This works especially well for coloured linen.

LIPSTICK

+ Stains will disappear if rubbed very lightly with a cloth moistened with white vinegar.

+ Or soften the stain with a little eucalyptus oil, dab with a few drops of ammonia and then rinse.

MILDEW

+ This is hard to remove. Rub with laundry soap, then put salt on both sides of the cloth and spread out in the sun. Repeat the process if necessary.

OIL

+ Cover with a paste of sugar and water.

PAINT

+ Paint can be removed from washable clothing with a mixture of equal parts of ammonia and turpentine. Rub spots with the mixture and then wash in heavy soapsuds.

+ Hot white vinegar will remove paint from cotton clothing.

PENCIL MARKS ON WALLPAPER

+ Rub these off with a dry bread crust.

RED WINE

While the stain is still wet, sprinkle with salt, leave for an hour or so and then wash off with warm water.

+ Or cover immediately with soda water, then pour boiling water through the stain.

+ Soda water will also remove red wine stains from linen.

+ For dried red wine stains, sponge with warm water and borax.

RUST

+ For rust stains on white material, rub with lemon juice and salt, then bleach in the sun. Repeat if necessary.

SCORCH MARKS

+ Dampen these and then hang in the sun. If fabric permits, light scorching will usually wash out with chlorine bleach added to the water.

+ For heavier scorching and wool scorching, cover the mark with a cloth soaked in hydrogen peroxide, cover this with a dry cloth and press with an iron as hot as it is safe for the fabric.

+ Severe scorching cannot be removed as it means the fabric is damaged.

SWEAT

+ Add 1 crushed aspirin to the soaking water. Fresh stains can be sponged with ammonia and dried-in stains with white vinegar. If stains persist, dampen and sprinkle with pepsin and leave for 1 hour, then brush off and wash. Treat persistent odour by sponging with colourless mouthwash.

TEA AND COFFEE

+ Provided the coffee stain has not been thoroughly absorbed into the cloth, pour boiling water through the stain. If you haven't been quick enough to treat the stain at once, then mix equal parts of egg yolk and glycerine, spread over the spot and left to dry. When the mixture has dried, wash in the usual way.

WHITEWASH OR DISTEMPER

+ Dab with a few drops of white vinegar.

WOOL BLANKETS

+ To remove stubborn stains, soak blankets for a short time in a packet of Epsom salts dissolved in warm, soapy water.

CLOTHES LINE

+ Use bulldog clips instead of clothes pegs to hang out sleeping bags, blankets or **heavy items** of clothing and they won't fall off the line.

+ Dry delicate articles on the clothes line without leaving **peg marks** by placing a sock from the wash between the garment and peg. It saves pegs because, of course, the socks also dry! Similarly, use old tights between pegs and T-shirts so they dry without peg marks and retain their shape. This keeps ironing to a minimum as well.

+ If **rain** threatens to soak the washing on the line, drape a lightweight, clear plastic, all-purpose protection sheet over the top of the line and peg it down firmly at each corner. Plastic sheets are cheap to buy and particularly useful for people who don't have a tumble dryer.

+ When you wash a dress with **shoulder pads**, dry it on a padded coat hanger. The dress keeps its shape and is much easier to iron. The shoulder pads will retain their rounded shape for longer, too.

+ **Chenille** bedspreads and dressing gowns should be washed on a sunny, windy day. Hang them inside out so that, when they blow in the wind, the chenille on one side fluffs up the pile on the other.

+ To dry **make-up sponges** and powder puffs, place them in an orange net or a pair of tights and peg on the line to blow in the wind. This prevents damaging them with peg marks and allows them to dry on both sides at once.

+ When washing **woollen** cardigans and jumpers, place an old curtain over your clothes line, then stretch the woollen garment to shape over it. This allows the air to circulate both over and under the garment for quick drying.

+ A good way to dry **heavy woollen garments** is to place them in a fitted sheet pegged tightly at both ends to form a 'hammock' for the garment to lie flat in. Delicate woollens can be spun gently in a salad spinner before hanging out – it's surprising how much water this removes without stretching the knitwear.

+ Hang your **pillowcases** on the line with the open end up. Not only do they dry quicker, but you'll also have a handy pocket to carry socks and underwear indoors.

+ Save time sorting loads of dry washing by buying inexpensive, stackable **laundry baskets** for each member of the family. You can then sort the clothes for each person straight from the line into their own basket. They can put their own clothes away and the empty baskets stack neatly inside each other for easy storage.

+ Slip a straight petticoat over a **pleated skirt** and hang them on the line together. The skirt will not blow about and the pleats will stay in place longer. Once the skirt is dry with the pleats in place, carefully twist it around and around and then store in an old stocking to keep it neatly pleated.

+ Protect your **tights** when hanging on the line by threading them through a slip or nightie or similar garment.

+ Hang **children's clothes** on the line inside out so that the hems are exposed to the sunlight. This way they will be less noticeable if and when you have to let the hem down.

+ When washing a dress with **puffy sleeves**, pad out the sleeves with plastic shopping bags and they will dry in a good shape.

+ After washing a child's **doll or teddy bear**, dry it on the line in an old string bag or nylon stocking.

+ If you don't have an outdoor area and live in a unit or apartment, but would still like to air dry your laundry, ask permission to attach a **towel rail** to the ceiling of the balcony. Then you can hang washing to dry on coat hangers, which takes up little space.

+ To make a simple **indoor clothes airer**, turn a baby's wooden play pen on its side or strip the cover off an old umbrella and enamel the frame and handle – suspend it and hang small items on it to dry. It can easily be folded away when not in use.

+ **Wooden pegs** will last longer if first brought to the boil in a pan of hot water and then dried. This brings out any stains in the wood and saves clothes from being marked, and prevents the pegs cracking.

+ When drying garments **indoors**, peg a plastic bag around the lower half to collect the drips.

+ A plastic pot plant holder with a chain, tied to the clothes line, makes a good **peg container**.

IRONING

+ Starch the **ironing board cover** every time you wash it to give a smoother ironing surface. It will also stay clean longer.

+ To make ironing easier on your legs and back, set the board to half height, pull up a chair and **sit down to iron.**

+ Keep a **spray bottle** of water nearby when ironing. If a garment becomes too dry to iron, just spray it a little.

+ Don't use too hot an iron for pressing **woollens** (and they should be 'pressed' rather than ironed – this means lifting the iron up and down often, rather than gliding it over the fabric).

+ When ironing a **pleated skirt**, use clothes pegs or hairpins to hold the pleats you've ironed. They make the job much easier and are also useful when storing pleated clothing.

+ For a neat sharp crease when ironing **trousers**, rub the inside of the crease with soap before pressing.

+ Before pressing **ties**, slip in a piece of thin cardboard cut to shape. This prevents seam marks from showing through.

+ When ironing a delicate **hand-embroidered** tablecloth, press the embroidery on the wrong side over a towel so the braid stays flat.

+ Lacy jumpers or **delicate hand knits** can be ironed more successfully under a sheet of dull brown paper, instead of a damp cloth.

+ Avoid damaging **fancy buttons** by holding a spoon over the button and ironing around it.

+ Hang **towel rails** on the inside of your linen-cupboard door for hanging ironed tablecloths. It keeps them neater than a drawer and saves having to iron them twice.

+ To remove **brown marks** from an iron, rub with steel wool and any household abrasive while the iron is still warm. Wash thoroughly with water to remove the residue. If your iron is sticky with starch, while it is still warm, rub it over with a towel that has been sprinkled with talcum powder.

+ To remove the creases and wrinkles from **posters**, set your iron to normal temperature, place the poster upside down on a flat board, spray lightly and evenly with fabric starch and iron.

Woollen laundry liquid

+

Combine 4 cups soap flakes (shred bars of soap on a kitchen grater), 1 cup methylated spirits and 1 cup eucalyptus oil. Bottle and label. This will set into a stiff flaky mixture, so should be stored in a wide-necked jar. To use in a spray bottle, add 2 cups boiling water and stir until the flakes dissolve.

MANCHESTER

+ If you have a partner who rolls over in bed and takes the whole **double doona** with them, sew flaps of short lengths of sheet along the side seams of the doona cover. Now, when you make the bed, tuck the flaps under the mattress. This will keep the doona in place.

+ For people with **cold feet**, instead of folding all the blankets back at the top when you make the bed, fold one back at the bottom, over the foot area. This makes tucking in easier as well.

+ If you have two or more bed sizes in your house why not mark the sheets with a single initial to differentiate between **sheets**. No more unfolding sheets to find the right ones, but make sure you fold the sheets with the letter showing. If you have room, label one shelf for each size of sheet, then you can find them even more easily.

+ You don't need to buy **pillow protectors**. To prevent stains on pillows, slip on an old pillowcase, then put the good pillowcase over the top. The old pillowcase needs washing only occasionally.

+ To turn flat sheets into **instant fitted sheets**, gather the corner of the sheet, pull it right down and over the mattress corner, place an elastic band around the sheet and tuck it under the mattress. Do this for all four corners of the bottom sheet and lower corners of the top sheet.

+ For an inexpensive **bedspread**, buy a pretty sheet during a sale, and edge it with lace, velvet or fringe.

+ **Electric blankets** can be stored between mattress and bed base in the summertime. This keeps the blanket flat and stops the wires getting twisted. Or roll it around a cardboard cylinder. The cord can then be pushed inside the cylinder and each roll wrapped in plastic.

CLOTHING

CLOTHING HINTS

+ Do you have a **zip that keeps sticking**? Try rubbing it with a bar of soap – it works every time.

+ If you live by the sea, you might find clothing zips stick because of the salt in the air. Simply **spray zips with furniture polish** from time to time to make them run smoothly, being careful not to get the polish on your clothing.

+ An easy way to **remove lint** and the remains of tissues from washed clothes is to rub them with a furry tennis ball when they are completely dry. If they are clothes you generally iron, rub with the tennis ball before ironing.

+ If you have **dog hairs** on your clothes – or any other bits of fluff for that matter – simply slip on a rubber glove and brush them off. It works wonders.

+ To clean dust, fluff and cottons from **dark garments**, use a piece of coarse cotton net (for curtains) and brush in an upward movement.

+ A plastic foam brush from the hardware store makes an excellent **clothes brush**.

+ To keep a **pure silk blouse** looking like new, don't hang it up to dry after washing. Instead, give it a short spin, then fold it into a dry towel, leave it overnight and iron dry with a cool iron.

+ To prevent **fly zips** slipping down, especially on jeans, tie a small loop through the tag on the zip and, when the fly is closed, slip the loop around the waistband button, then button the jeans. The zip will stay up and you won't be able to see the loop under the fly of the jeans.

+ Snip small pieces from the **inside seam** allowance of special-occasion clothes; put these on a safety pin and carry them in your bag for when you are buying accessories and matching colours.

+ To stop a **slip** from clinging to your dress, wear the slip inside-out.

+ A soiled **leather** (but not suede) coat can be cleaned at home if it is guaranteed waterproof. Rub with a warm damp cloth rubbed in saddle soap. Any greasy parts can be scrubbed with a nailbrush. All soap should be thoroughly rinsed off with warm water.

+ A suit or coat that has developed **shiny patches** can be improved by brushing with a solution of 1 teaspoon ammonia mixed in 500ml warm water.

HATS

+ If the brim of a **straw hat** becomes limp, stiffen it by pressing with brown paper and a hot iron. A felt hat brim will improve if pressed under a slightly damp cloth, but do beware of shrinkage.

+ If a **straw hat** is dull, old or has lost its gloss, try giving it a quick once over with hair spray to enhance its shine.

+ Wash out and reuse large circular ice-cream containers as **hat stands**. You can keep the matching accessories in the container.

+ To keep a natural raffia hat with an open weave securely in place on a windy day, use wooden kebab skewers as **hat pins**. They blend well with the material of the hat and you can cut them to whatever length you need.

SHOES

+ **Store** suede, leather or plastic shoes in sealed plastic bags into which you have sprinkled Epsom salts. They will not show any sign of mould or mildew even after a long time in storage.

+ To clean **Ugg boots**, spray them with a pre-wash solution and leave for 30 minutes. Then make a slightly stronger than usual solution of wool wash and scrub them well with a stiff brush. Don't over-wet them: just dip the brush into the solution. Hang the boots on the line to dry, then spray 2–3 times with waterproofing solution.

+ To clean **black satin shoes**, sponge with white vinegar.

+ Save money on expensive shoe polish for cleaning brown leather: use the inside of a **banana peel** instead. It works just as well and can be thrown into the compost afterwards. Just rub on, then polish off with a cloth or brush for a deep shine.

+ **Shoe polish**, when dried out, can be gently warmed until it melts and reforms. If very dry, mix with a little cooking oil while it's still hot. Or soften polish by adding a little turpentine or vinegar. Cover polish with a piece of plastic wrap under the lid to keep it soft.

+ Before polishing shoes, cut back the polish build-up by rubbing with an old sock dipped in **methylated spirits**; then polish as usual and they'll shine like mirrors.

+ Clean **patent leather** shoes and handbags with Vaseline to preserve and protect the patent.

+ Put **shoe polish** on your shoes and leave overnight. Rub up the next day and your shoes will remain polished longer.

+ To dry **wet shoes** without harming the leather, place the nozzle of your hairdryer inside each one for a few minutes. Stuff them with newspaper to absorb the moisture and help them dry in shape.

+ Plain court shoes can be given a glamorous evening look by adding inexpensive **clip-on earrings** to the front of them.

+ If your **elastic-sided boots** are too tight around the ankles, push in a soft drink bottle (the size will depend on how loose you want the boots) and leave there for 2 weeks. Hey presto, the boots should now fit perfectly.

+ Use white correction fluid to cover **scuff marks** on children's white sandals. It can also be used to camouflage scuff marks on the toes of white shoes before you polish them.

+ **Gumboots** are a problem to store. Drive some stakes into the ground at the back door and upend your boots over them when you go inside. Rain can't get inside them and any moisture in them can dry out. Creepy crawlies are also kept out. A convenient gumboot stand can also be made by inserting two tight-fitting lengths of dowel into the central holes of a house brick.

+ To make it easier to get **gumboots** on and off, line each one with a plastic grocery bag and they'll just slip on and off.

+ Use an old toothbrush to **remove sand** stuck inside shoes.

+ Soften **water-hardened** boots and shoes by rubbing kerosene into the leather. It will make them as pliable as new.

+ If you're ready to go out but have forgotten to polish your shoes, simply grab a tissue and some **hand lotion** and give them a quick buff. You'll soon get the sheen you're looking for.

+ Felt-tipped marker pens, available in many colours, can be used to touch-up **scuff marks** on handbags and shoes.

+ Nail a metal bottle top to the back of a shoe cleaning brush so it can be used for scraping away **caked-on mud**.

+ Slip an old sock over your hands before cleaning **sandals** to protect your hands from polish or cleaner.

+ To restore **discoloured** brown shoes, paint them with iodine, allow to dry, then polish in the usual way.

+ Raw oatmeal will effectively clean **pale-coloured suede** shoes. Rub into the suede, leave overnight then brush off with a soft brush.

+ Steel wool is a good substitute for a wire brush to **clean suede shoes**.

+ Renovate worn **suede** shoes by holding them over a steaming kettle. Leave to dry, then buff briskly with a suede brush.

+ To revitalise **suede** shoes that have become shiny, dip a toothbrush in white vinegar, brush over the suede and allow to dry.

Shoe polish

+
Bring 1 cup linseed oil to the boil in a double boiler. Cool, then gradually add 1 cup white vinegar. Store in a glass jar and clearly label as shoe polish.

Smelly shoes

+

If your trainers have grown smelly, spray inside them with hair spray. Leave to dry, then sprinkle in a little talcum powder and the bad smell will disappear forever.

+

Eliminate odour by dusting inside the shoe with a small amount of bicarbonate of soda before wearing.

+

Remove odour by sprinkling powdered herbs into your shoes each evening – use dried camomile, hyssop or pennyroyal, and reduce to a powder by rubbing through a fine wire sieve.

+

Alternatively, mix sufficient aromatic oil, a drop at a time, with bicarbonate of soda and sprinkle this in your shoes.

+

When you take off your trainers, put a bar of soap in each one. You'll have no more smelly sports shoes and your feet will smell great.

WARDROBE

+ Hang a moth-repellent **cedar ball** on each coat hanger in your wardrobe by a ribbon loop attached with a drawing pin; you can add small flowers to pretty them.

+ When you need a **skirt hanger** and you can't find one, use a plain wire hanger and two spring clothes pegs instead.

+ Stitch old **shoulder pads** onto both ends of fabric coat hangers to help your jackets and dresses hang beautifully and stay in shape.

+ It is easy to make damp collectors to reduce **mould** and odour in drawers and wardrobes caused by moisture in a humid climate. Put 4 tablespoons bicarbonate of soda in a paper bag, fold one end to close it, and then seal with sticky tape. Place the filled bag where it's needed and replace every 6 months or so.

+ Instead of using expensive **plastic garment bags** to store blankets and woollens, firstly wash or dry clean them, then add your choice of moth repellent and parcel up in airtight paper packages, sealing the joins with packing tape. Label well.

+ Sprinkle cinnamon oil on cotton balls and place in drawers instead of **mothballs** when you are storing woollies. It does the job and smells much nicer. Dried cloves in the pockets of jackets and coats when you're storing them will keep moths at bay and leave a lovely aroma.

+ Store woollens in new, unwashed, unbleached **calico bags**. Moths will not attack garments stored in this way.

+ To keep **white woollen articles** white, store them in a pillowcase that is regularly washed with a good amount of laundry blue.

HOUSEHOLD
CLEANING

HOUSEHOLD CLEANING HINTS

+ To remove **grease spots** from anything, mix 1 part cloudy ammonia with 1 part water and sponge over the spot.

+ To **clean photographs**, just rub a slice of soft bread over the surface to revive the appearance.

+ Marks on **wallpaper** come off if rubbed gently with stale bread, then wiped with Dettol on a damp cloth.

+ To clean **fabric wallpaper**, dab with baby powder, leave for 2 hours, then gently brush off.

+ To **protect and maintain leather**, boil 550ml linseed oil with 275ml white vinegar and apply with a soft damp cloth.

+ To give a professional finish to **leather goods**, clean well, then apply egg white and allow to dry. Polish off with a soft cloth.

+ **Cleaning ceilings** can be a messy business. To prevent water and detergent dripping down on you and the furniture, cut a cross in the middle of a large plastic bin lid and secure it with tape to the middle of a squeegee mop handle. This will catch all the drips.

+ To **clean drains**, lift the grid off occasionally, flush with boiling water and caustic soda (following the packet instructions) and scrub the sides of the drain. Remove any clogged material from the hole leading to the main drain. Finally, sprinkle with chloride of lime from the chemist. Wear gloves and handle chemicals with care.

+ To clean smoke and soot from brick **fireplaces**, rub with neat white vinegar or make a paste of cream of tartar. Spread on the smoke stain, leave to dry, then brush off.

+ Badly stained or **blackened brickwork** can be cleaned with a solution of hydrochloric acid from the hardware store or chemist. Mix 1 part acid with 5–6 parts water and brush carefully over the surface of each brick, keeping the acid off the cement. Rinse thoroughly with plenty of water. The acid is poisonous, so use with care and wear gloves.

+ To clean **alabaster**, wash with warm water and soap, then dry well and polish. Stains can generally be removed by rubbing well with a piece of cloth dampened and dipped in fine scouring powder.

+ Unless you keep a drip tray under your car, **oil** is likely to stain the garage floor or driveway. If the stain is fresh, clean up as much as possible with a rag, then sprinkle the stain with sand or powdered cement. Leave for a while, then brush up the sand and scrub the stain with detergent and water. If the stain is old and dried-in, you may need a commercial concrete cleaner.

+ Whether finished or not, the best way to clean **cork** is with a detergent solution. If burns or stains have penetrated the cork, sand them out with fine sandpaper. Lacquered cork will need re-finishing after that. If the cork is chipped, grate a bottle cork into tiny slivers with a kitchen grater and make the chips into thick putty with clear lacquer shellac. Use this to fill the dents and sand smooth when dry.

+ To clean a **crystal chandelier**, place a plastic cover and a few sheets of newspaper over a table under the chandelier. Fill a glass with lukewarm water and add a dash of white vinegar or alcohol. Hold the glass up to each crystal teardrop and immerse it, then allow it to drip dry.

+ Clean **plastic piano keys** with warm water and a little white vinegar.

+ Clean **ivory piano keys** with a solution of half methylated spirits and half water.

+ To **clean interior paintwork**, first clean with sugar soap and then use a little bicarbonate of soda, white vinegar or cloudy ammonia on a damp cloth.

+ For greasy **household brushes**, use liberal amounts of washing soda as well as soap. Dip the bristles in the soapy lather and rinse thoroughly in warm water to remove the soap residue. Rinse in cold water, shake to remove excess water and hang outside to dry.

+ Clothes and **shoe brushes** should not be overlooked when cleaning household equipment. Use warm soapy water.

+ Sponge **gold picture frames** and ornaments gently with white vinegar for a perfect clean.

+ Dip an old toothbrush in bleach and use it to scrub hard-to-reach **corners** in cupboards and windows.

+ Use a baby's hairbrush, a pastry brush or any other small brush to dust **fragile ornaments** – it will get into all the nooks and crannies.

+ When Ugg boots or sheepskin slippers are worn out, don't throw them away. Cut out the soles, wash the sheepskin in the washing machine and you are left with a great **polishing cloth**.

+ When opening a new bottle of **disinfectant**, use a skewer to pierce a hole in the lid. This gives the bottle a 'squirt' action that reduces the amount of disinfectant you use. When you buy the next bottle, swap the caps.

+ Leave a metal skewer in your household **cream cleaner** bottle. The opening at the top will never get blocked and the cleaner won't dry out.

+ If your **vacuum cleaner** has a dust bag that must be emptied, put the open end of the dust bag into a strong paper bag, large enough to allow it to be shaken easily. Then shake the vacuum cleaner bag into the paper bag without dust flying everywhere.

+ A small dish of salt on a windowsill will help soak up **condensation**.

+ If **flies** bother you in your house, hang bunches of mint in different rooms. This will drive the flies away and leave your house with a garden-fresh smell.

·RECIPE·

All-purpose spray cleaner

+

Mix 1 teaspoon borax,
1½ teaspoons washing
soda, 2 tablespoons white
vinegar, 2 tablespoons
cloudy ammonia and
¼ teaspoon liquid soap
in a spray bottle and add
2 cups of very hot tap water.
Shake very gently until the
ingredients have dissolved.

BLINDS AND LAMPSHADES

+ Scrub **holland blinds** with a soft brush dipped in detergent and water and then hang out to dry. If your holland blinds are getting thin and shabby, a coat of plastic paint on each side will make them smart again.

+ Clean **venetian blinds** by putting your hands into a pair of woollen socks as if they were gloves. Rub the slats with both hands. If the blinds are very dirty, dampen the socks with methylated spirits or cloudy ammonia in a little water.

+ Clean **parchment lampshades** by rubbing them all over with fine dry oatmeal on cotton wool. Discard each piece of cotton wool as it gets dirty.

+ **Fabric lampshades** can be cleaned by dipping in warm soapy water and then rinsing in warm water. Hang to dry in the breeze, out of the sun.

+ Curtain blind and light **cords** can be cleaned by rubbing with white shoe cleaner – use the type that has a sponge dispenser that you can run along the cord. The cord will stay clean for a long time and can be freshened up in seconds.

+ To clean dust from **fly wire screens** without removing them, put on a pair of rubber gloves and, from the inside of the house, rub all over the screen with both hands. Watch the dust come free and fall to the outside windowsill to be wiped up.

BRASS

+ Clean brass by rubbing with the cut side of half a **lemon**.

+ To remove **verdigris** from brass and prevent it forming, dip half a lemon in salt and rub the stain with it until all the green is removed. Wash in warm soapy water and dry well.

+ When you've cleaned brass, finish with a light covering of **hairspray** and the shine will last for months.

COPPER

+ Clean copper with half a **lemon** dipped in salt. Rub the lemon and salt over the surface, then rinse off immediately with water. The copper should polish up beautifully with a dry cloth.

+ Remove marks from unlacquered copper with a dry cloth dipped in **white vinegar** and salt. Rub hard, then wash and polish.

+ To clean **verdigris** from copper ornaments and utensils, rub with a mixture of 1 tablespoon kerosene and 1 tablespoon bicarbonate of soda. Rinse and dry.

CARPETS AND RUGS

+ Use soda water to remove **red wine** from a carpet. Cover the stain with soda water immediately, then cover with an old towel. Do not rub, but press down firmly (even standing on it) to absorb the liquid. Repeat until the stain is removed. It is also a good idea to have the carpet shampooed as soon as possible.

+ Bicarbonate of soda is a cheap **deodorant** for carpets and upholstery and works especially well on pet smells. For even distribution, use a flour sifter to sprinkle the bicarbonate over the area. Vacuum off 15 minutes later.

+ Floor rugs should be turned around occasionally so they get **equal wear**. Wall-to-wall carpets cannot be removed, but furniture should be moved around occasionally to even out wear. All carpets should be regularly vacuum cleaned and rugs beaten to remove grit, which damages the pile.

+ To remove a **furniture dent** in carpet, leave an ice cube on it overnight. In the morning, brush to restore the pile and the dent will have disappeared. You can also use a coin to rub up the pile. Alternatively, cover the pile with a damp cloth and steam gently, but quickly, by placing a hot iron on top of the cloth.

+ When you have **new carpet** laid, keep some off-cuts to use for repairs later on. To repair a hole, slide a piece of plywood under the damaged area, place the new section of carpet over the old and hold it firmly, being careful to match the direction of pile and pattern. Then cut through both layers at the same time with a sharp knife. Seal the edges of the new piece with carpet adhesive. Remove the plywood and place the new patch into the hole: it should be nearly invisible.

Vacuum hints

+

Add a handful of dried herbs to your new vacuum cleaner bag for a beautifully scented home, or moisten cotton wool with essential oil or fragrant oil and place it in the bag. Try placing a deodorant block, or handful of mothballs or flakes in the bag.

+

If animal hair is difficult to remove from the carpet while vacuuming, wear rubber-soled shoes and rub them over the carpet as you walk. This creates matted balls that you can vacuum up easily (while simultaneously toning your legs!).

+

Place a tissue over the dust filter of your vacuum cleaner to collect dust and hairs. Keep changing the tissue and your filter will last longer.

+

After cutting a flea collar to fit your cat or dog, don't throw away the excess. Pop it in your vacuum cleaner bag to kill any insects or fleas sucked up during vacuuming.

+ To get rid of **moths** in carpets, thoroughly clean the carpet with a vacuum cleaner, then lift it up if you can and allow to air outdoors. Under-felt should be treated the same way. Scrub the floorboards thoroughly with hot soapy water with added disinfectant.

+ To stop a rug **slipping** on a polished floor, attach some latex from the hardware store to the back of the rug.

Carpet cleaner

+

Add ½ cup pure soap flakes to 5 cups boiling water and boil for 1 minute. Add 3 tablespoons washing soda and 3 tablespoons cloudy ammonia, pour into a spray bottle and label clearly.

FLOORS

+ White vinegar is a mild **natural disinfectant** that cuts through grease and soap build-up on a kitchen or bathroom floor. Add ½ cup white vinegar to every ⅓ bucket of water. Better still, tip a little vinegar onto the floor and wipe over with a damp mop.

+ Just a capful of **linseed oil**, added to the washing water, will improve the appearance of wooden floorboards and give them a lovely shine.

+ To clean floors, including cork tiles, ceramic tiles, lino and slate, add 1 cup **white vinegar** to each ½ bucket of warm water.

+ To clean **slate floors**, dip a polishing cloth in milk and wipe over the tiles. Buff off with a clean soft cloth or polishing cloth. Or wash with hot water with a capful of car wash added: it brings a lovely shine to slate and gives a slightly wax coating.

+ Scuff marks from shoes on **vinyl floors**, which usually take hard scrubbing to get off, can be easily removed with a little eucalyptus oil on a tissue.

+ If hot **candle wax** drips onto your wooden floor, suspend a plastic bag filled with ice cubes over the wax to harden it. When it is solid, ease off the wax with a blunt knife, then rub the wood with a soft cloth to remove any film. Now apply a little liquid polish to the cloth and buff well. Where heat marks have occurred, rub along the grain with ream metal polish (this can be made by as a paste of vegetable oil and salt).

+ Fountain **pen ink** can be difficult to remove from wood floors, especially if it is an old stain that has gone unnoticed. Using a cotton wool bud, gently dab with neat household bleach. Blot with kitchen towel and repeat if necessary. Always use quick dabs of bleach because rubbing the area will leave white spots on the wood.

All-purpose floor cleaner

+

Mix together 1 cup white vinegar, ½ cup cloudy ammonia, 1 cup washing soda, a few drops of lavender oil (optional) and 2 litres hot water in a bucket, then use to mop floors.

FURNITURE

+ Save old nylon stockings for **dusting** furniture: the static attracts dust particles.

+ Olive oil or eucalyptus oil will remove spots from **leather furniture**.

+ If **leather furniture** is marked with a ballpoint pen or correction fluid, clean off with eucalyptus oil. Dab the oil on the stain with a soft cloth and gently rub. Rinse with warm, soapy water and dry well.

+ If there is **chewing gum** on your upholstery, and it is still soft, rub an ice cube over it until it hardens, then scrape as much off as you can with a dull knife or putty knife.

+ To clean **cat hairs** from upholstery, use a damp piece of foam rubber as a brush. If your broom refuses to pick up hairs, tack a strip of foam rubber to the back of your broom head. Then you just turn it over to pick up the hairs.

+ Make your own **upholstery cleaner** by mixing washing-up liquid with a little water. Whip into a froth and skim off the bubbly foam. Use this foam to clean the upholstery without soaking, so that it dries quickly. Always test a hidden part of the upholstery first to check for colourfastness.

+ To clean **cane furniture**, wash with lukewarm, salted water, rinse and dry, then gently rub over with linseed oil.

+ To clean **padded cushions** on cane furniture, remove all dust with a furniture brush or suitable vacuum cleaner nozzle. Wash the case with warm soapy water, trying not to soak the cane. Rinse with cold water and dry outside.

+ Disguise cracks and chips on **black furniture**, ceramics and so on with black nail polish.

+ The cut side of a freshly cut **apple** will remove ballpoint pen from vinyl furnishings. Cut the apple in half and rub briskly until the stain is gone, then wipe the area gently with a clean, damp cloth.

+ Revamp a **sagging lounge** or sofa bed by placing 4cm-thick high-density foam, cut to size, underneath the seat cushions. You'll be surprised at the extra comfort for such little cost.

+ If you have to replace furniture on a **freshly cleaned carpet** before it is completely dry, put drinks coasters under the legs. This prevents stains, indentations and rust marks.

+ To **re-web a chair**, it is essential to pull the webbing as tight as possible. Use a block of wood about 15cm long and 2–3cm thick as a web stretcher. Tack the webbing to one side of the chair, bring to the opposite side, wrap it around the block and press the wood firmly against the chair. Push the block down to make the webbing really taut. Tack down, cut and nail again in three places.

JEWELLERY

+ To **untangle necklaces** that have twisted together in a drawer, sprinkle with talcum powder and they will come apart.

+ Hang all your **necklaces** on a small tie rack in the wardrobe. They're easy to see and stay neat and tidy.

+ Use a kitchen mug tree to store **necklaces and bracelets**. It stops them getting tangled and looks pretty on your dressing table too.

+ A good way to keep your **earrings** in pairs and easy to find is to hook them onto a piece of lace and hang it from the mirror in your bedroom.

+ Fix a small cup hook on the wall near the sink to hold **rings, watches and bracelets** safely while washing up.

+ If you wear **copper** rings or bracelets, paint the insides with clear nail varnish to prevent skin discolouration.

+ **Clean jewellery** in a solution of detergent with warm water. A soft toothbrush cleans the back of stones.

+ For beautiful, shiny **clean gold and diamonds**, use a soft toothbrush and toothpaste. Rub lightly, rinse and polish with a towel.

+ To **clean rings**, squeeze a small amount of toothpaste into the palm of your hand, then rub the ring between your hands for several minutes. Rinse the toothpaste off and polish with a soft cloth.

+ To **clean gold jewellery**, soak in a little cloudy ammonia for 5–10 minutes. Rinse in clean water. Dry with a soft cloth.

+ **Clean gold jewellery** by rubbing between your hands with small pieces of fresh bread. When you rub the bread it will form small balls and clean the jewellery.

+ To **clean silver jewellery**, put 500ml water, 2 teaspoons washing soda or bicarbonate of soda and a piece of aluminium foil in a pan and bring to the boil. Immerse the jewellery in the pan using a strainer. Dip in and out a few times and shake in the boiling solution. Rinse and dry on a soft towel.

+ To **clean diamonds**, mix a small quantity of soap, hot water and a few drops of cloudy ammonia. Scrub lightly. Remove and then dip in alcohol for the final shine.

+ **Clean pearls** by placing them in a plastic bag with a handful of dry uncooked rice and shaking the bag. The rice will polish the pearls and bring back their lustre.

+ Polish **coral jewellery** with a drop of vegetable oil on a soft cloth to restore the coral's lustre.

+ **Marquisate jewellery** can become very dull. To bring back the sparkle, rub a stick of white chalk lightly over the stones. Polish with a small dry brush and then rub gently with a soft cloth. To clean, rub with soft tissue paper.

+ To **clean copper jewellery**, wash in warm soapy water, then dip the jewellery in a solution of 2 parts white vinegar and 1 part salt. Dry with a soft cloth.

SILVERWARE

+ Rub **bicarbonate of soda** on silver and then wash in hot soapy water. Dry with a clean cloth.

+ To clean **stained silver cutlery**, place 2 teaspoons salt in 500ml boiling water in an aluminium saucepan and leave the cutlery in this for several minutes.

+ To keep silver spoons and forks in **good condition** when not in use, wrap in aluminium foil or a ziplock bag.

+ To keep silver cutlery bright, save the **moisture-absorbing sachets** that come in postal parcels with shoes, medication etc and keep them in the cutlery drawer. The sachets absorb the moisture, so the silver doesn't tarnish as quickly. You might need several sachets, but they work well and you won't need to polish the silver often.

+ A block of **camphor** in the drawer will absorb moisture and prevent silver tarnishing.

+ To prevent silver salt shakers turning green with **moisture** from the salt, paint the inside of the screw top with clear nail polish.

+ Stainless steel cutlery that has **dulled** can be brightened again, by using a soft cloth dipped in lemon juice to rub each piece. Then wash in a bowl of hot, soapy water with 1 tablespoon bicarbonate of soda added and dry well.

+ To **clean silverware**, line a large pan with aluminium foil, fill it with warm water and add ½ teaspoon washing soda. Add the silverware and leave for 30 minutes. Or place the silverware in an aluminium pan, fill with boiling water, and add 1 teaspoon soap powder. Add the silverware and leave for 30 minutes. A few drops of methylated spirits in the water adds sheen to the silver.

Silver cloths

+

Mix 1 tablespoon Silvo and 2 tablespoons cloudy ammonia in 2 tablespoons hot water. Wring out soft cloths in the mixture and use as tea towels for drying silver.

WINDOWS

+ Scrunch up **newspaper** into a ball, dip in white vinegar and use to polish your windows. Wipe dry with clean, dry newspaper.

+ Always save **newspapers** for cleaning windows and to buff the dry glass: the printers' ink gives extra sparkle.

+ If you still have copies of **White or Yellow Pages**, save them for tearing up and buffing glass – they have the added advantage of not blackening your hands with newspaper ink.

+ Add ¼ cup white vinegar and 1 teaspoon cloudy ammonia to 2 litres water to make an excellent **window cleaner**. Keep in a bottle and use on a clean cloth for sparkling results.

+ Make a strong brew of **tea** by putting 6 tablespoons tea leaves in a bucket and filling with boiling water. Allow to cool and strain off the tea leaves. Polish your windows with the liquid, then wipe off with a clean soft cloth.

+ Mix 2–3 tablespoons **white vinegar** or cloudy ammonia in 4.5 litres water. Soak a sponge or chamois in this solution and wring out, then wipe over the whole window. Then take a whole soft toilet roll and use as a pad to wipe the damp window, or hold the rubber blade of a squeegee against the top of the glass and draw it all the way down to the bottom. Lift the squeegee off and wipe over with a chamois, drying the squeegee after each stroke. Work in one direction on the outside, and cross-wise inside so that you can see if you have missed any.

+ When cleaning window frames or sills (or any difficult corner areas), use a 2.5cm **paintbrush** dipped in moderately hot suds.

WOOD

+ To repair **scratches** in wood, mix 1 tablespoon olive oil with 2 teaspoons white vinegar and apply with a dry soft cloth.

+ To disguise any small **scratches on dark wooden furniture**, rub with the edge of a brazil nut. On light or coloured woods, fill the scratch carefully with shoe polish or wax crayon.

+ To remove **heat marks** from wood, rub with a mixture of 1 teaspoon salt and 2 teaspoons olive oil.

+ To remove **candle wax** from a polished wood table, gently scrape off as much as possible without scratching, then soften the rest with a hairdryer set on low heat. Use a soft kitchen towel to remove, then polish as usual.

Wood cleaner and polish

+

Mix ½ cup strained lemon juice with ¾ cup olive oil in a plastic screw-top bottle and label. To use, shake well and apply with a soft cloth – this is a very effective cleaner for asthmatics as it picks up dust instead of flicking it into the air. To clean odd corners or carved areas, apply the mixture with an old shaving brush or toothbrush.

Wood restorers

✦

To restore old wood furniture, mix equal parts methylated spirits, linseed oil and white vinegar. First wipe the furniture with a cloth wrung out in warm, soapy water, then rinse and dry. If the furniture still seems soiled, rub with a cloth dipped in a little mineral turpentine, before re-polishing with the restoration mixture.

✦

To restore old wood furniture, mix equal parts white vinegar, linseed oil and pure turpentine. Add 1 teaspoon white granulated sugar to each 285ml mixture and shake well. Use as a cleaner as well as a polish and rub off with a soft cloth. This removes dirt and gives an 'antique' look.

PETS

DOGS

+ If you feed your dog vegetables, add 1–2 teaspoons **crushed garlic** when you're cooking them. Garlic helps reduce flea infestations.

+ Add pennyroyal, eucalyptus or tea tree oil to plain pet shampoo to control **fleas**. When washing your dog, add a couple of capfuls of eucalyptus oil to the water. The oil is a natural flea repellent that makes a great alternative to chemicals, and it's also gentle on your dog's skin.

+ Potted fennel near a dog kennel will keep **fleas** away.

+ Suction pads used for holding bars of soap in place by the sink are also great at securing **pet food bowls** to the floor.

+ To make a cheap **outdoor pet bowl** that won't blow away in high winds, fill an ice-cream container with 2cm sand. Then sit a container of the same size on top of the sand.

+ Banish **ants** from your pet's food dish by wiping the floor under and around it with a cloth dipped in kerosene, then stand the food dish in a larger dish of water.

+ Put your dog **kennel** on wheels; it can be easily rolled around so it won't kill the grass and can be moved under cover in bad weather.

+ If your dog has to wear a **bandage** on a paw and keeps chewing it off, spread soap on it.

+ Remove **grass burrs** from a dog's coat by first crushing the burrs with a pair of pliers – the pieces will then comb out.

+ Mothballs placed in the garden will prevent **stray dogs** from coming in to do their business. They last for several weeks.

+ Adhesive tape is very effective in removing **pet hair** from fabric. Wind a length, sticky-side-up, around three fingers. Brush the tape over the hairs until no more hairs are sticking to the tape. Do this several times to finish the job.

+ The easiest way to wash a small dog is in a **wheelbarrow**. You don't need to bend over much and, after bathing, it acts as a table for drying the animal.

+ To keep dogs from knocking over lightweight plastic bins, stand them inside old car tyres. A few drops of eucalyptus oil on top of the **rubbish bin** will also deter dogs.

PUPPIES

+ If your new puppy **cries at night**, try putting a loud ticking clock wrapped in an old fleece or cardigan in the basket – even better if you can wear the clothing for a while first. The clothing keeps him warm and smells of you, and the ticking of the clock keeps him company.

+ To deter a puppy from **chewing the legs of furniture**, wipe a little oil of cloves on the furniture legs (do a patch test first).

+ To clean **urine stains** made by young pets, soak up as much as possible with newspaper spread over the stain, then apply a mixture of 3 parts water, 1 part white vinegar and a few drops of detergent. Leave for half an hour then rinse with water and pat dry.

CATS

+ At mealtimes, if your cat turns up its nose when you put out canned food, try giving it 10 seconds in the **microwave** – the food, not the cat!

+ To keep your cat's **litter tray** smelling sweet, crush some dried herbs with the litter. Lavender, rosemary or rose geranium are all great deodorisers.

+ If you are spending a lot of money on **kitty litter** for your cat's tray, buy a 40kg bag of pony pellets from a stock feed store instead. This is used by most catteries, is a much cheaper alternative and doesn't leave any odour.

CHILDREN

BABIES

+ When you're pregnant with your first baby, it is hard to know which baby products are the best value for money. Try contacting companies and asking for **samples**. Most companies will send them out and then you can decide which products you prefer before your baby is born.

+ When **bathing** your very young baby, wear a cotton glove on the hand you are using to support them. This helps you keep a firm hold when they are slippery with soap and water.

+ When your baby outgrows the **baby bath** but is nervous of the big bath, pop the baby into a plastic clothes basket placed in the big bath. Your baby will feel secure, the toys won't float away and, in no time, baby will be used to being in the big bath. Remember to never leave a baby alone in a bath.

+ Cutting baby's **fingernails** can be nerve-wracking at first, because it can be easy to nick their skin. Put a little talcum powder in the palm of your hand and gently rub baby's fingers through it. The tips of their nails will fill with powder, letting you easily see how far to cut.

+ An easy way to put **drops** in a baby's eye is to lie them down and shine a torch on the ceiling (for a small child, they can hold and direct the torch themselves). The light spot absorbs their attention and, as their eyes follow the beam, the drops will circulate well.

+ To help babies sleep comfortably when they have a **cold**, place cotton wool soaked in eucalyptus oil near, but out of reach of, the cot.

+ To keep a baby's **bottle** warm in winter, place it in a stubby holder. It insulates very well. (Stubby holders are beaut in summer, too, for keeping an older baby's bottle cool!)

+ **Freeze boiled water** in sterilised ice-cube trays – one block is usually 10ml. Then, if you are filling a baby's bottle and have made it too hot, just drop in a couple of blocks. This cools the liquid quickly for that impatient hungry baby.

+ In very hot weather, fill a hot-water bottle with iced water and place it in baby's cot or bassinette to **cool the bedclothes** before putting baby to sleep.

+ Help your baby to **sit securely** by putting a blow-up swim ring around their waist, instead of propping them up with pillows. It will save a lot of toppling over and bruising!

+ Keep your baby amused by hanging an assortment of toys, teaspoons, paper butterflies etc on a clothes horse. Now you have a good-value portable **amusement centre** you can move around the house with you. Take care the baby can't reach anything and topple the clothes horse over.

+ A plastic bucket is an excellent way to **carry baby and toddler toys**. You can take the bucket of toys with you when you visit friends or when you move from room to room in the house. It's about the right size, brightly coloured and inexpensive, with a perfect handle.

+ Cut a few simple **shapes**, such as stars, fish or animals, from old thin kitchen sponges, and push them into a clean, empty soft drink bottle, then three-quarters fill the bottle with water and replace the lid tightly. Place the bottle on the floor and your baby will have hours of fun rolling it from side to side and watching the shapes swimming.

+ Mix 1 teaspoon full-fat **cream cheese** with any bottled or canned food your baby doesn't take to. They will often then happily try the food they initially rejected.

+ Commercial **baby food** can be expensive for those on a limited budget. As well as blending your own steamed vegetables, why not buy large cans of unsweetened fruit and blend them? You will generally get 8 to 10 serves for the same price as 3 cans of baby food.

+ Getting a toddler to eat can sometimes be tricky; try putting a **glove puppet** on your hand and let the puppet feed your child.

+ When **shopping** with your baby in a pram, you can carry bags by looping Velcro strips around the pram handle and through the bag. Make sure your bag is never heavy enough to overbalance the pram!

+ Attach a cup hook to a baby's high chair to hold **bibs**.

+ Instead of buying costly **highchair** spill mats, use a flannel-backed tablecloth: it's both cheap and easy to clean.

+ A square of plastic under the **highchair** will catch food, spoons or toys that inevitably drop.

+ A professional's hint: when taking a **photograph** of a baby or toddler, you will capture great expressions by blowing bubbles over their head.

+ Cut away the feet from old socks and use the sleeves as knee protectors when a baby is learning to **crawl**.

+ An empty ice-cream container, attached to the central arm rest of the car by two loops of wide elastic threaded through holes in the base, make an ideal box for a child's small toys on **long car journeys**.

+ Fill an empty perfume bottle with disinfectant and pop it into your baby bag. It's very useful for spraying over **public change tables**. Better mark the bottle clearly, though – otherwise a careless squirt on your clothes could have you smelling like a changing mat.

+ When you no longer need your child's **cot**, remove the drop side, cover the mattress with a bright fabric and add some cushions to make a useful seat in your child's room.

TODDLERS AND YOUNG CHILDREN

+ For **toilet-training** little boys, put a ping pong ball in the toilet bowl as a target to aim at. It will reappear, of course, after flushing. This focuses his aim and keeps the drips off the floor.

+ When you're **moving house**, pack the children's rooms into the truck last and reconstruct them first when you arrive at your new home. Having their room organised and familiar will make it easier for them to adjust to a new home.

+ Place an extra handle on a **screen door** at your child's level so they can let themself in and out, saving you from having to open the door every 5 minutes, or leave it open, letting in flies and insects. Of course, this is for a back door only, into a fenced garden, without access to roads or pools.

+ Crush **medicine** tablets for children in 1 teaspoon icing sugar.

+ To avoid pain when a child has a **splinter**, apply a dab of teething gel to the spot before using the needle and tweezers. It completely numbs the area.

+ Small children often find it difficult to learn **left and right**. Help them recognise the capital L plainly made by the thumb and forefinger of the Left hand.

+ For children who are afraid of the **dark**, stick luminous stickers around the light switch. This also helps parents find the light switch in the middle of the night.

+ A lovely way to keep your child's special **paintings** is to add the name and date, then laminate both sides and use them as placemats.

+ To avoid squabbles in the bathroom, supply each child with matching coloured face cloth and toothbrush. That **colour** then becomes the child's own, so they can identify and use their own things. As they get older you can do the same with swimming towels, bath towels and so on (making it easy to spot the person who isn't hanging up their wet towels!).

+ When siblings are inclined to **compete over food** and are reluctant to share, allow one to cut the food and the other to choose the portion. They will quickly get very good at cutting the portions evenly!

+ Children playing in the **back seat of a car** can cause a driver to lose concentration. Use elastic bands to fix a long, narrow mirror to the back of the sun visor, so that you can keep an eye on them easily. They can make eye contact with you, too, and will behave better.

+ To remove **chewing gum** from a child's hair, try applying cold cream or eucalyptus oil to the area. Leave for a minute, then pull a dry towel firmly down the hair strand. The gum should slide away.

+ Personalise **hand-me-down** clothes from friends or siblings by adding new buttons or appliqués. It's even better if the child selects the new trimmings themself.

+ Encourage young children to eat their lunch sandwiches by using a teddy bear or gingerbread man **biscuit cutter** to cut them into shapes. Add currants or sultanas for eyes.

+ To hide children's ballpoint scribbles on **wallpaper**, use correction fluid. Lightly tint with a colour from a child's paint set that matches the wallpaper. This should disguise the marks very successfully.

+ Children who kick off their **bedclothes** and get cold during the night can be kept warm and cosy by loosely tucking a double blanket around them. This allows them freedom of movement without them ever becoming completely uncovered and losing body heat – the same concept as the expensive children's 'sleeping bags' you can buy for babies and toddlers. To go one better, make up a child's bed with a full-size blanket. The blanket tucks further under the mattress and can be used later when the child grows and graduates to a larger bed.

+ A small **bell** sewn to toddlers' slippers will let you know where they are, when you are busy cooking or doing things around the house and can't have your eye on them all the time.

+ Collect all your cardboard off-cuts, cardboard tubes, bottle tops and milk cartons and drop them into your local preschool. The children can use them for arts and crafts while you're **recycling**.

+ If your child constantly gets out of **bed** at night with the excuse that they want a drink of water or a cuddle or whatever, try making them a small decorated card and call it a Bed Pass. This entitles the child to get out of bed *once* for any reason. Maybe, if the child saves up the passes, they can be redeemed for a special reward at the end of the week.

+ **Shoe laces** won't come out if a knot is tied on each side, after the lace has been threaded through the two last holes.

+ If a child is learning to **knit**, use two different coloured needles: one for the plain row and the other for the purl row.

+ Whenever you are sitting on a crowded beach, tie a colourful **balloon** to your beach bag, deckchair or beach umbrella, so that the children (both big and small) can easily find you. Buy the new compostable brands now available.

+ To help prevent children getting lost on **crowded caravan and camping sites**, tie a balloon with a long string to the top of your van or tent. They'll be able to find their way home easily. Buy the new compostable brands now available.

+ If you have guests for dinner and you don't have enough room at your table, use your **ironing board** as a temporary table. Put the board up halfway and children can use it while sitting on the couch.

+ Tuck in the corners of **tablecloths** when small children are about; it could save an accident.

+ For young children, write **phone numbers** on the backs of photos of family and friends and fit them into albums to make an illustrated phone book for an emergency. Keep this by your home phone.

+ If your home phone stores numbers, put **coloured stickers** on the numbers of close friends and relatives. This way, in an emergency, a child can get help. Be sure to explain the stickers and have a test run.

Don't lose it!

+

For permanent labels on school clothes, write the name on strips of iron-on interfacing; once ironed onto the garments they'll never come off. Or label school clothes and bags with fabric paints. The paint is permanent after drying for 24 hours, doesn't fade and won't come off. Don't forget to label shoes, which seem to be easily lost and are often very expensive to replace. Write your child's name and phone number inside with permanent marker.

PLAY TIME

+ If a **teddy bear** has suffered too much love and is starting to come apart at the seams, use dental floss instead of cotton to sew it up. Floss is stronger and more pliable than cotton and can handle the toughest love.

+ If you own a number of **jigsaw puzzles**, the pieces can often get mixed up, which can be exasperating and hard to spot. So the first time you complete a new puzzle, turn it over and colour the back of the pieces with coloured felt pen. Then mark the box with the same colour.

+ Save the screw caps from toothpaste tubes to use as **counters** in children's board games. Little fingers can manage them more easily than the usual small, flat counters that come with the games. You can watch out for coloured ones, or colour them yourself with pen.

+ Coat new **boards** for games with clear self-adhesive book covering. They will last longer and can be wiped clean after playing. The instruction books can be covered as well, for a longer life.

+ Cut the legs off a pair of laddered tights and use them to store children's wooden **jigsaw puzzles**, assembled. The stocking hugs the puzzle and keeps it intact, and you can easily see which puzzle is which.

+ If your children love **books**, why not make some. Glue different pictures (cut from old magazines) into a scrapbook and give each page a different heading, such as: Colours, Animals, Shapes, TV Characters and Alphabet. Not only is it educational, but you can get your children involved by asking them to sort pictures and suggest their own themes.

+ Cut the numbers from old calendars and store them in a small cardboard box. Small children can make a game of **matching numbers**, while older children can learn their times tables by racing to group numbers.

+ A good idea for keeping young children amused on a rainy day is to make a **photo album** especially for them. Use duplicates of your favourite shots of family, pets, outings and so on. The children will get hours of fun from it.

+ To entertain children indoors, put a **tennis ball** inside an old stocking or tights leg, hang it from a hook in the ceiling and give them room to hit the ball with tennis racquets. It will keep them amused for hours.

+ A game of Snakes & Ladders played with young children can be a long drawn-out affair that loses its appeal. Use **two dice** instead of one. It moves the game along and teaches them to add up.

+ If your small child loves undressing their **dolls** but sometimes can't get the tight-fitting clothes back on, sprinkle some talcum powder over the doll's upper legs and you will find that the difficult clothes slip on easily.

+ Make a toddler's disposable **painting apron** from a plastic grocery bag. Cut across the sealed bottom, then split up the back. Put the child's arms through the handles and tie at the back. Make children's cooking aprons by cutting head and armholes into old pillowcases.

+ An oven mitt makes an excellent **blackboard duster**. Children love using it, it can be hung from a small cup hook on the blackboard and it can easily go in the washing machine.

+ Preschoolers love **painting** when the paint is put into cleaned, refillable, roll-on deodorant containers. Mums love the lack of mess!

+ Add a few drops of glycerine to soapy water when children are **blowing bubbles**. The bubbles will be larger, stronger and more brightly coloured.

+ A good **sandpit** for children is a large truck tyre filled with sand. Cover the tyre with a weighted board at night.

+ Plastic trellis makes an effective cover for a child's **sandpit**. It discourages cats and other inquisitive animals, yet is light enough for children to remove by themselves.

+ When children are still playing at the end of the day, set a **timer bell** to give them a 10-minute warning that teatime or bedtime is near. When the bell rings, they need to wind down their activity and pack up. A 15-minute buzzer might better suit older children.

+ **Balloons** make great, cheap bathtime toys for playing with your toddlers. Buy the new compostable brands now available. Fill a balloon with water until it fits in the palm of your hand, tie a knot in it and you have a semi-floating toy that toddlers love. You can also fill a balloon with air – it makes a great sound when slapped on the water and will burst to the surface when released from below. They last for weeks without going mouldy.

PARTY TIME

+ When making **jellies** for children, use only half the hot water required, then finish diluting with fizzy lemonade. It gives a good tingly taste that children love.

+ Instead of buying expensive commercial **party bags**, buy inexpensive cake boxes and fill them with a picnic tea. Then hand out crayons, paints and stickers and other decorations, to make a picture that the guests can take home in their box with cake, sweets and crayons.

+ Make **place cards** using different-coloured balloons (buy the compostable brand) with guest names written on. They're much more effective that ordinary cards and the children can take them home at the end of the party. Push a wrapped lolly into the neck of each balloon before blowing it up – then there are no tears if the balloon bursts.

+ As a cheaper alternative to **helium balloons**, use double-sided sticky tape to stick groups of balloons to walls and ceilings.

+ If you want a **birthday cake** but your child doesn't like cake, make a simple ice-cream cake. Buy a tub of ice cream, make sure it's well frozen, then remove from the freezer and leave in a bowl of hot water for a couple of minutes, so that you can turn it out onto a plate. Decorate it as you would a party cake, adding a paper frill around the side and sticking sparklers on top. An instant hit!

+ If your small children usually only eat the **decorations** from their birthday cake, make a whole large cake from chocolate crackle mixture. Draw a shape (teddy bear, or number) on greaseproof paper placed on a tray. Spoon the mixture onto the shape and decorate with coconut for a fuzzy teddy bear, or pipe with icing for other features.

+ Try a little homemade **magic** at your next party. Put drops of various food colourings in the bottom of clear tumblers, carry them into the party empty and on a dark tray to hide the drops. Pour in clear lemonade and different coloured drinks will magically appear.

+ Use sheets of butcher's paper for the party **tablecloth** and have several boxes of crayons handy. This will keep the children happily entertained between eating. (This is also fun at adults' drinks too!)

+ If you are worried about the expense and work needed for a children's birthday party, hold a birthday **sleepover** instead. Your child can invite four friends over to watch movies, eat party food and play party games – ask them all to bring a pillow and sleeping bag. They could sleep on the floor of the lounge room or, when old enough, they love to sleep in a tent in the yard. The cost and organisation are minimal, but best of all the children love it and will probably ask for the same on their next birthday.

CHRISTMAS

CHRISTMAS HINTS

+ Keep a notebook with you during the year to jot down Christmas **present ideas** for family and friends. It will make the job much easier and prevent last-minute panic-buying.

+ Don't throw away the **net bags** that contain oranges. Instead, cut the tops off, thread a Christmas or tartan ribbon through the raw edge and fill with little gifts and sweets for an inexpensive Christmas stocking.

+ Use an oven bag to line your **Christmas pudding** basin. When the pudding is cooked, simply lift it from the basin and store until Christmas, or decorate the bag and give as a lovely gift to a friend. Puddings should be replaced in a basin (still in the oven bag) for heating on Christmas Day.

+ Ask your greengrocer for any spare polystyrene boxes to use as practical **coolers** for storing drinks and salads at hot Christmas barbecues.

+ Take a photograph of your children opening each Christmas gift sent by friends and relatives far away. Use the snaps as **thank-you notes**.

+ Instead of throwing out an old **wall clock**, take off the clock hands and put a photo inside behind the glass. It makes an interesting photo frame and a great Christmas gift.

+ When Christmas is over and it's time to scrub the **fake snow** off your windows, simply spray it with oven cleaner and leave for 5 minutes. It will then come off easily when you wipe it with a wet rag.

+ Next year, try writing your **Christmas cards** in September! You will be more relaxed and have the time to write that extra special personal message. It will also give you pleasure to see the cards all ready and waiting to be posted.

+ Always be on the lookout for gifts at **garage sales**. You can often find bargains; toys and games at a fraction of the price of new ones. Sometimes all that is needed is a few minor repairs or a new coat of paint.

+ These days, with many artificial Christmas trees and decorations, the lovely **Christmas smells** of pine resin no longer permeate the air. Recapture that evocative aroma with essential oils. Simply spray a fragrant oil mixture, such as pine oil and water, or sprinkle a few drops of the same oil around the base of the tree. A few drops of oil on a piece of material wrapped around the trunk is also effective.

Festive house perfume

+

Dissolve 8 drops mandarin oil, 4 drops tangerine oil, 2 drops cinnamon oil and 2 drops frankincense (optional) in 10ml methylated spirits. Add to a pump spray bottle containing 500ml distilled water and spray throughout the house to give it a Christmas aroma.

TREE DECORATIONS

+ If Christmas **lights** are always tangled when you get them out, leaving them in danger of fusing, ask at an electrical store for a discarded cable spool. The lights wind onto the spool without damaging the globes. Alternatively, wrap them around a cardboard roll (such as a Christmas wrapping roll).

+ If you have small children and boisterous pets, stop them toppling the Christmas tree by putting it in a baby's **playpen**.

+ Old **light bulbs** make good Christmas tree decorations. Save them during the year, paint them in bright colours, scatter with glitter and add a hanger. They show up against greenery and are very effective.

+ If your **silk-covered** Christmas tree balls are past it, simply strip them, cover them with glue and roll them in glitter.

+ For a cheap and effective way to decorate a Christmas tree, thread **popcorn** on long lengths of cotton and twine around the tree like tinsel strands.

+ Christmas decorations can serve a dual purpose. First you can use the **baubles and tinsel** to add sparkle to wrapped gifts, then, when everything has been unwrapped, you can hang them on the tree.

+ Hold onto empty **egg cartons** – they make excellent storage for small fragile Christmas tree baubles.

+ Glittery **earrings** that no longer have a mate can be recycled as Christmas tree ornaments – they already have a hook!

+ When the **stand** of an artificial tree has seen better days, replace it with the base of an old pedestal fan. It is secure and looks very smart.

WRAPPING PAPER

+ Have a length of string with your wrapping paper when you're wrapping Christmas presents. If you're unsure how much paper to cut from the roll, quickly wrap the string loosely around the package. Use this as a handy **measuring guide** to gauge how much paper to cut.

+ Wrap Christmas gifts in pretty **fabric and ribbon** offcuts from your local haberdashery store. It works out much cheaper than wrapping paper and, what's more, it won't break and tear!

+ If you run out of wrapping paper, use **aluminium foil**. No sticky tape is required and awkward shapes are a breeze to wrap. The presents are silvery and shiny under the Christmas tree when the lights are on.

+ Instead of throwing out old Christmas **cards**, cut the pictures from the cards, pierce a hole in the top corner with a hole punch or skewer and thread with ribbon to make gift tags for next year.

+ An interesting alternative to using expensive Cellophane for wrapping Christmas gifts or baskets is to use **oven bags** with a bit of ribbon.

+ As soon as Christmas is over, hit the **sales**. Buy plain, coloured or metallic Christmas wrapping paper when it is cheaper and you can use it all year for birthday and wedding presents. You can also buy your Christmas paper and cards for next Christmas at half price – and buy presents when you see likely items. It's amazing how much money can be saved this way.

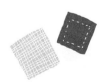

SEWING,
KNITTING
AND CRAFT

SEWING HINTS

+ Always look out for small repairs and mend them **immediately**.

+ A **needle** is easier to thread if you spray a little starch, beeswax or hairspray on the end of the thread first.

+ To prevent cut **ribbon** from fraying, dab clear nail polish on the ends.

+ When making plain **curtains** (not those with pinch pleats), make the hems at the top and the bottom the same. The curtains can then be turned upside down to spread the wear evenly.

+ To renew **elastic** quickly in waistbands, ankles or cuffs, just attach the new elastic to the old in the garment with a safety pin, then pull out the old elastic. The new elastic will follow through as you pull.

+ Put safety pins at both ends of the **elastic** when threading it through a waistband. That way if either end disappears into the waistband it should be easy to find and work it out again.

+ When sewing a **hem by hand**, tie off the thread every now and then and begin again, so that if the thread breaks the whole hem doesn't come down.

+ Fasten a **safety pin** to the tag of shorts, skirts, shirts and dresses. If your hemline unexpectedly drops, you'll be prepared.

+ To **adjust the hem** of a dress if there's no one around to help you, hang the dress over another one on a hanger. You can then pin the hem using the dress underneath as a guide.

+ Make a warm rug quickly and cheaply by **recycling** unwanted woollen cardigans and jumpers. Mark squares about 20–30cm on undamaged sections of the garment and sew around the edge with zigzag stitch. Then cut out and stitch the squares together, using a loose tension and a long stitch on your sewing machine. Stitch again for added strength. Join strips of squares in rows, then line the back with a piece of flannelette or cotton.

+ Use **shirring elastic** instead of cotton wherever buttons are put under extra strain, such as children's clothes.

+ Stitch on the lowest **button** of button-through dresses or uniforms with fine shirring elastic instead of cotton. This allows plenty of give and prevents the bottom button tearing from the material.

+ When hand sewing with **double thread**, tying a knot in the end of each thread will prevent the two threads tangling.

+ If you are sewing on a button with **four holes**, sew through one pair of holes at a time. Then if one thread breaks there is a chance that the other will hold until you can do repairs.

+ To keep **spare buttons** neat and tidy, thread them onto a large safety pin.

+ You can prevent **bra straps** slipping off your shoulder under a sleeveless dress. Cut an 8cm length of ribbon and sew a press stud fastener on either end. Sew one end to the dress at the shoulder seam. When you put the dress on, put the bra strap under the ribbon and hold it in place with the press studs so it can't slip off your shoulder.

How to disguise a let-down hem

+

Let-down hems usually have a tell-tale crease. To make this
disappear, mix 1 cup warm water, ½ teaspoon white vinegar
and ¼ teaspoon borax. Soak a cloth with this and press over the
hem line, with a warm iron, on the wrong side, until nearly dry.
Brush gently on the right side.

+ Stitch or glue a length of **velvet ribbon** to the underside of a shoulder
bag strap to prevent it slipping off your shoulder.

+ If velvet has **creased** while being sewn, hold it over a dish of steaming
water for a while, or rub it over the wrong side with a chamois rung
out in hot water.

+ **Reinforce** children's jumpers and pants on the inside of elbows and
knees with patches cut from nylon stockings.

+ Small pieces of material for **patching** or alterations are easily found if
they are kept in clear plastic bags. Wash patches and dry on the line
before sewing, to help them match the worn garment.

+ Before sewing **leather patches** onto clothes, sew around the patch
with the machine unthreaded, then hand sew. The machine holes will
be neat and even and the needle will slip through easily.

+ **Patches or appliques** can be stitched quickly if backed with thick
starch, ironed in position until dry, and then machine sewn.

SEWING KIT

+ Glue golf tees to the bottom of a shoebox to store **cotton reels** neatly, preventing the awful tangle that can happen when they are thrown together in a sewing box.

+ To keep cotton reels at your fingertips and prevent them unravelling in your sewing box, store them on a **wire coat hanger**. Unwind the twisted end of the coat hanger until it's open, slip your reels over one end and re-twist the coat hanger closed. Hang in your sewing area and simply unwind the cotton as needed without removing the reels from the hanger.

+ When sewing on buttons, if you don't have any **button thread**, you can make your own. Run ordinary cotton around a candle or beeswax several times before threading your needle. The wax coating makes the thread extra strong. It also stops it knotting and tangling. You can use dental floss to sew on buttons, too. For extra strength, dab a little clear nail polish in the centre of the button.

+ Keep a small **magnet** in your sewing box so you can easily find lost pins or needles. Simply tie it to a piece of string and trail it around your work area, or poke it into the odd corners of the sewing machine.

+ When travelling, an empty **lipstick case** is a convenient container for pins and needles.

+ Fill your **pincushion** with steel wool to keep pins and needles sharp.

+ Warm **scissors** before cutting nylon material. It seals the edges and prevents fraying.

+ It is always hard to get a **sewing pattern** back into the envelope without screwing it up or tearing it. Why not place the pattern in a plastic pocket instead, add the envelope as a 'label' and keep in a ring binder of patterns.

+ **Tattered sewing patterns** can be restored by pressing iron-on interfacing to the worn sections and trimming. The notches and edges of dress patterns can then be re-cut easily.

+ Sheer fabrics are easier to sew if you first push the pins and needles into a bar of **soap**. This makes a film on them so that they won't slip, no matter how flimsy the material.

+ When taking up a hem, use **paper clips** instead of pins. The result is a firm hem with no pin marks.

+ Prevent damage to a garment when cutting off a button by sliding a **comb** between the fabric and the button. A comb can also be used as a spacer when sewing on a button that needs to stand out from a garment.

SEWING MACHINE

+ Fix your sewing **instruction sheet** on the wall near the sewing machine with Blu-Tack. You can then follow each step without getting the sheet in the way of your fabric and it will come off the wall without leaving a mark.

+ Use a small paintbrush with a drop of **oil** on the tip to clean the bobbin area and working parts of your machine. The brush will oil the parts and collect dust and fluff at the same time.

+ Glue a length of **tape measure** to the front edge of the sewing machine and coat it with clear varnish. It is useful for checking measurements while you are sewing.

+ The eye of the sewing-machine **needle** is easier to see if you place a piece of white paper under the machine foot when threading the needle.

+ To check the **tension** on your machine, thread the bobbin with one colour and the top needle with another. It makes it easier to see which needs adjusting.

+ For neat even **gathers** in material, loosen the tension on the machine and stitch two parallel rows. Draw up the two threads together from the back and fasten tightly.

+ A handyman's box with clear plastic **drawers** is good for holding buttons, fasteners and other small items.

+ A plastic shoe bag with rows of **pockets** makes a useful holder for storing bias binding, tapes and odd pieces of mending material. Hang it up by your machine.

+ A small **bag** attached to the side of your sewing machine makes a useful container for waste lengths of thread.

+ Hold on to large **padded postal bags**: they're great to use as a mat under the sewing machine to protect the table and prevent slipping.

MENDING CLOTHES

+ Prolong the life of children's **tracksuits** when they become too short in the arms and legs by inserting contrasting bands of fabric to lengthen them.

+ When the feet of toddler **all-in-one sleep suits** wear out, cut off the sock section at ankle length and sew on an ordinary pair of socks, preferably in a size large enough that they are loose fitting while the child sleeps.

+ Children's **winter pyjamas** can be lengthened by letting down the hems of pants and sleeves and adding the tops of worn stretchy socks, turning them into cosy ski pyjamas.

+ Overalls and trackpants that have become too short for your child can be **lengthened** with knitted cuffs in a rib of 1 plain, 1 purl sewn to the bottom of the legs. In a toning colour, they look attractive, hug the ankles and provide extra warmth.

+ When a child outgrows a **favourite t-shirt** with a picture on the front and is sad to stop wearing it, cut out a square from the front of the old t-shirt and sew on to the front of a new plain-coloured t-shirt.

+ **Towels** wear out in the centre. Cut out the good parts and sew them into babies' bibs, nappies or hand towels. Fold a long rectangle of towel in half and sew up the two sides to make a handy oven mitt.

KNITTING HINTS

+ When using a set of **four needles** for knitting, use a different coloured one for the first row of each set, then you will know when each round is finished.

+ To knit a hollow tube to cover a **coat hanger**, cast on an even number of stitches, then knit one and slip one in every row. Make sure you knit the slipped stitch of each previous row. Hey presto: a seamless tube!

+ To **remember** how many rows you have knitted when you knit the same pattern from top to bottom, thread a needle with a different colour, then make a loop through, say, every tenth row. This makes counting easier.

+ Instead of using a **stitch counter**, keep a child's abacus near you to count rows. It's easy to move one of the beads with an empty needle.

+ If you're **unravelling** some knitting to use the wool again, wind it around a filled hot water bottle — all the crinkles will come out.

+ If you slide a ball of wool onto a **kitchen towel holder** it will unwind as you knit.

+ When **unwinding** a ball of string or wool, start pulling from the middle instead of the outside, and you'll avoid knots.

+ As you **unpick wool**, rewind it on to an extended skirt hanger, then wash it and hang it up to dry.

+ It's often hard to remember which is the **right side** when knitting certain patterns, so mark the right sides of the pieces with a length of contrasting coloured wool until the pieces are sewn up.

+ When knitting or crocheting from a pattern with multiple sizes, use a **highlighter pen** to first mark all directions for the size you are making. Then you can see immediately how many stitches are needed. If you want to make a different size later on, use a different coloured highlighter.

+ When you've finished sewing up a hand-knitted garment, tack a little leftover wool along the inner seam. It'll come in handy for **repairs**.

+ When knitting a **buttonhole**, knit into the back of each stitch on either side. This gives a nice, firm buttonhole.

+ To save taking a newly knitted garment to the shops to find the right **buttons**, knit a small square, including the appropriate sized buttonhole, and take that instead.

+ When you have knit a **baby jacket**, use one long strand of wool to sew on all the buttons by threading it through the back of stitches. Then there's no worry about buttons coming off.

+ When threading ribbon through knitted **baby booties**, double back one ribbon hole in the centre at the back to prevent the ribbon pulling out and getting lost.

+ When making a knitted toy that requires a **base** to stand on, cut the base from a thin plastic item, such as an ice-cream container, rather than cardboard. A plastic base will not disintegrate when washed.

+ When knitting a **neckband** on four needles, you'll get a more even job if you knit two or three stitches from the next needle at each needle change. This means you never change needles at the same place and so avoid the gap that can show at the end of each needle.

+ Change to smaller needles for the **shoulder** shaping when knitting a jumper or cardigan for a narrow-shouldered person (which older people often are). This will ensure a better fit.

+ **Lengthen** knitted jumpers and skirts by cutting a stitch a few rows above the basque or hem. Unweave the row and pick up the stitches. Knit the extra length required, in stripes or contrasting colour, if the original wool is not available.

+ **Worn elbows** of hand knits can be repaired with a knitted square hand-sewn over the worn area, before a hole has worn through.

+ If you want to mark a row in a pattern, snap in a **press stud** and you can see at a glance where it is.

+ When **sewing together** the pieces of a knitted garment, use a long knitting needle to pin the straight edges together first. Then pull it away as you sew.

+ Stuff knitted toys and nursery balls with old **tights or stockings**.

+ Line a knitted **beanie** with the top part of a pair of tights. It stretches to fit the head and doesn't pull the hair out of place when taken off.

+ When doing wool **embroidery** on a knitted garment, tack a firm piece of cotton material to the wrong side and work through both thicknesses to prevent the wool stretching.

+ To keep **white woollens** spotless, press, hang and store garments inside out.

+ If a child's knitted garment is becoming too short, add a **crocheted border**, perhaps in a contrasting colour.

Plastic mats

+

Use plastic shopping bags
to make attractive and practical floor
mats. Cut around the bag in a continuous
10cm strip and wind this into a ball.
Collect enough bags to make several
large balls of plastic yarn. Using large
knitting needles and garter stitch, knit a
mat to the required size. These are
great in the bathroom or as
quirky door mats.

KNITTING KIT

+ Cardboard post **cylinders** with lids can be recycled as excellent
  containers for your knitting needles.

+ Don't throw away empty **wet wipe containers** – they're ideal
  for keeping string or wool nice and tidy, and to stop it from
  unravelling too far.

+ To keep knitting needles neat and tidy, slot them into **curtain tape**, then roll them up and tie with a ribbon. Or use corrugated cardboard: thread the needles in graduated sizes into the 'tubes' in the cardboard, write the size next to each pair, roll and secure with a rubber band.

+ Ordinary **pins**, even glass-headed pins, can get lost when sewing up knitting, but the pins used to secure plastic hair rollers do a wonderful job. They're easy to see and remove when the garment is complete.

+ When teaching **young children** to knit, it's easier for them to learn if you give them two crochet hooks. Using the hook end as the needle point, and they won't lose the stitches, or their patience, as often.

+ Paste much used knitting or crocheting **patterns** on cardboard to prevent tearing or creasing.

+ A good **present** for someone who's a keen knitter is a range of knitting needles. Choose a different colour for each size and she or he will be able to select a pair at a glance.

+ If you get **sore hands** when doing crochet, buy a squash ball and pierce two holes in it with a skewer, then push the hook through to a comfortable position. The ball will not move and instead of trying to handle the narrow hook, you can manoeuvre the squash ball.

+ Knitting needles will glide smoothly through the wool if they are rubbed with **furniture polish** and then polished.

+ When knitting with more then one strand of wool, thread each through the holes of a button to prevent **tangles**. A colander also does the same job.

CRAFT HINTS

+ Collect large, fallen autumn **leaves** to use as invitations, gift cards, place cards or short notes for friends. Write your message on them with a felt pen.

+ Use pages from old magazines to make quirky personalised **envelopes** for letters or cards. Make a template from a commercial envelope, lay it on the magazine page and cut around it. Fold and glue in the appropriate places. Use white sticky labels for the address and return address, so they can be seen clearly by the post office.

+ Art **paintbrushes** are expensive and need protection when not in use. If you lose or damage the protective tube the brush was bought in, then make a substitute from a drinking straw cut to the right length and split down one side. Shape the paintbrush head to a point and pull, handle first, through the straw until the tip is covered.

+ If you wet the **string** before tying a parcel, you'll find the knots stay firm after the string has dried out.

+ If you have little jars of **glitter** that get spilled easily, pour the glitter into a bottle of clear glue. It's easier to use and goes much further.

+ When you have a pile of beautiful wrapping paper from a celebratory occasion, such as a wedding or christening, keep it to line **drawers** in your bedroom as a happy reminder of the day.

+ Cut a **tiny picture** of each family member (from group photos) and stick them on the appropriate birthday date on a calendar for a cheerful reminder. It makes a lovely gift for grandparents or children.

+ To dye white **artificial flowers**, use methylated spirits to which the required amount of food colouring has been added. After dipping the flowers, dry them on clean brown or white paper.

Glue tips

+

When gluing small things together, use bulldog clips as a clamp. For larger items, metal kitchen tongs with a sliding clip work well, as they extend wider.

+

Before using a new tube of glue, grease the inside of the cap with cooking oil to prevent it sticking.

+

To prevent super glue drying out once opened, store it in the fridge. It will remain free flowing indefinitely

IN THE HOME

HOME HINTS

+ To keep your TV **remote controls** looking new, cover them with cling wrap. Pull the cling wrap tight and secure on the back with sellotape. It will protect them from drink spillages and sticky fingers.

+ To prepare for a **power cut**, always keep a torch and all sizes of fuse wire, wrapped in plastic, in the meter box. If you live in an area that suffers from long power cuts, keep a portable battery pack charged up to provide lighting when the power is off.

+ Placing a dish of ice cubes in front of an electric fan will cool down the house on **hot days**.

+ To carry something small or **fragile** that might be easily damaged in transit – such as a piece of cake or a flower – put the item in a plastic bag, then blow up the bag and then seal the top with a twist tie.

+ Keep a **safety pin** on your key ring. It comes in useful for almost anything.

+ A good way to keep **make-up tidy** is to use a cutlery tray in your bathroom or dresser drawer.

+ For an excellent **draught excluder**, buy a long woollen scarf from a charity shop, fold it in half and stitch it up the long sides and one end. Stuff it with used supermarket bags and sew up the other end. When it's dirty, simply empty it, wash the scarf and refill.

+ Paint clear nail polish over the hinges on **glasses and sunglasses** to prevent the tiny screws working loose and falling out.

+ If you are bothered by **flies** in your house, hang a bunch of fresh mint in every room to drive them away. It really works and leaves your house smelling garden fresh.

+ A few drops of lavender oil sprinkled about a **bookcase** will help keep your books free of mould.

+ Before putting guests in a stuffy, rarely used spare room, peel an **orange** and leave the peel in the room for several hours. It will leave it smelling fresh and sweet.

+ To sweeten a damp, musty **cellar**, place some charcoal on trays and put them in different parts of the cellar. Charcoal absorbs moisture.

+ A little Blu-Tack under the bottom corners of **picture frames** will keep them hanging straight on the wall.

+ If you need to refill a **beanbag**, try filling smaller plastic supermarket bags with the beads and then putting the filled bags in the beanbag. It's quicker and easier than having the loose beads sticking to everything. Alternatively, forget the beads and recycle plastic shopping bags by stuffing them into saggy beanbags. Just open the zip and keep stuffing the bags inside until the seat is firmly padded.

+ If you live in **rental accommodation** and can't hang pictures on the walls, brighten a blank wall with a coloured cotton or silk scarf. Attach Blu-Tack to the corners and press hard against the wall – it will stay in place.

+ The **ticking of a clock** on a bedside table can keep you awake. Cover the clock with a clear glass bowl – you'll be able to see the time without hearing the ticking.

+ A little furniture polish sprayed on wooden **curtain** rods will help the rings glide more easily.

+ To clean off the remains of **sticky labels**, sprinkle with talcum powder and rub with your finger, or dab on a little eucalyptus oil and rub gently.

+ Soak **doormats** in cold salty water to prevent the fibres falling out. Dry out before use. In hot weather, re-soak them again.

+ To prevent **static** shock, touch the article with a plastic biro first.

+ To find a dropped **contact lens**, stretch a pair of tights over the nozzle of a vacuum cleaner, then vacuum the room. The lens will be sucked onto the tights and you can lift it off easily.

+ Sliding doors and window **seals** are places where water usually gets in, so make a habit of cleaning the drain holes around the bottom of the doors to prevent rust developing.

+ When you replace the battery in your **smoke alarm**, attach a sticker with the date. That way, you'll know when it needs replacing (after about a year) and you won't get an annoying beep in the night as it runs low.

+ Tape a new long-life **battery** to the backs of clocks and smoke alarms. You'll never be caught out without spares if the battery runs down.

+ Before moving **heavy items**, such as fridges and washing machines, put on a pair of rubber gloves. They will give you a good grip and make the job a lot easier (you can also use them to open stubborn jars). Drag the item on a mat or blanket to prevent making marks on the floor.

+ Camphor **blanket chests** can lose their lovely aroma. If this happens, rub the inside of the lid with fine sandpaper and the smell will return.

Candles

✦

Candles will burn for longer if they are put in the freezer
for 1–2 hours before you light them.

✦

To prevent a candle dripping, stand it in a tall glass of salted water
for a couple of hours before use. Keep the wick dry,
of course, or the candle won't light.

✦

Spray inside candle holders lightly with cooking spray before
pushing your candles into them. After use, the wax left by the
candles pops out, making cleaning the holders much easier.

✦

Use a potato peeler to shape candles to fit your candlesticks.
You will end up with a smooth finish and snug fitting candles.

✦

To melt wax on the lower part of the outside of a candlestick, stand it
on newspaper and move a hairdryer (on a low setting) slowly back
and forth until the wax melts away.

✦ Put tacks behind the bottom corners of a heavy **picture frame**. Air
will then pass freely behind the frame and prevent ugly discolouration
where the frame usually touches the wall. Small strips of plastic foam
will do the same job and will keep the picture straight.

✦ In damp weather, when **doors** get stuck, rub a piece of hard soap or
the stub of a candle up and down the edge.

+ White **correction fluid** can be useful for touching up chips in white paintwork, such as vacuum cleaner marks on white skirting boards, etc.

+ An easy way to re-thread a **venetian blind** is to tape the new cord to the end of the old one and simply pull it through the holes in the slats and over the pulleys.

+ **Burglar-proof your doors** with wooden wedges. Slip them under doors, making them impossible to open except from the inside.

+ Make **casement windows** burglar-proof by drilling two holes through the top rail or the bottom sash, one at each end. Insert a 75mm screw into the lower rail with the window closed. The window can't be opened unless you remove the screw from the inside.

+ **To make an extra shelf**, if space allows, attach cup hooks into the shelf above and suspend the extra shelf with lengths of wire or string. Use for light objects such as spices in the kitchen, or magazines.

+ To make an inexpensive set of **bookshelves**, or shoe storage, use concrete building blocks for ends, with timber, masonite or glass as shelves. This can be added to as the need arises and needs no special installation.

+ The best way to **cut rubber** is with a wet sharp knife.

+ Use a piece of bread (the more processed and stodgy, the better!) or dampened cotton wool to pick up tiny fragments of **broken glass**.

+ A piece of cotton saturated with kerosene (paraffin) and placed inside a **clock** for a few days will often clean the works.

+ If your **chimney catches fire**, extinguish it by burning a handful of sulphur on a shovel held up the chimney. Or put a pile of wet newspaper on the fire. The steam from the papers will put out the fire.

+ If you are taking out an old **window pane** and the putty is hard, soften it with kerosene first. Leave the kerosene on for day – you might have to repeat the process over several days to penetrate and soften the putty.

+ If the **putty** around a window has dried out, causing the glass to rattle in the frame, ease a little candle wax between the frame and glass to solve the problem until you can renew the putty.

+ If you have **stiff windows or drawers** that are difficult to open, rub them with a candle, bar of soap, Vaseline, talcum powder or dressmakers' chalk. All will act as a lubricant.

+ If a **rug curls at the corner**, cut out an L-shaped piece of heavy cardboard and glue it to the underside of that corner.

+ To make a **stepladder more secure** and prevent the legs moving while you are on it, stick a piece of rubber on the base of each leg.

+ **Oil** machines when they have been running for some time and have warmed up. This helps the oil penetrate.

+ Clean all **steel tools** after use and wipe them over with an oily rag.

+ When **storing suitcases**, put an unwrapped bar of soap inside each one to prevent musty odours.

+ A rubber-headed tack on the back of a **chair** prevents it marking walls.

+ To **cut a ceramic tile** to fit an edge or corner, score the glazed surface with a tile cutter drawn once across the surface against the straight edge. Place a matchstick or nail under the scored line and press the edge down firmly. The tile should snap firmly in two. To cut a shape in a tile, 'nibble' out the desired shape with a pair of sharp pliers.

Window frosting

+

Sometimes you might need to frost existing clear glass windows for privacy. There are two ways to do this yourself. You can either paint the glass with a mixture of white vinegar and Epsom salts, or apply a thin coat of white oil paint.

+ You don't really 'cut' **glass** with a glass cutter: you score the glass to release the surface tension and then snap it along the score line. To cut glass expertly, place a T-square a fraction to one side of your intended cutting line, hold the glass cutter between your index and middle fingers and draw the cutter towards you. Avoid pressing too hard or going over the line a second time. Break the glass with pliers along the score line.

+ To store rubber-backed **curtains**, place them on the floor, rubber-side-up. Sprinkle generously with talcum powder and then fold them. This stops the rubber sticking together and perishing.

+ To store **lino**, roll up with the pattern on the outside, preferably around a wide cardboard tube. If no tube is available, roll the lino with as wide a diameter as possible. Stand the roll on its end and leave in a warm room for at least 24 hours before relaying.

PAPERWORK

+ Do you often misplace tax receipts, lottery tickets, theatre tickets, appliance instructions, council notes and so on? Try keeping them in a well-labelled A4 **clear document folder** or photo album.

+ In a safe place, keep a list of all the cards and vital information you carry in your **wallet** or handbag. If your wallet is lost or stolen you can contact the banks and relevant authorities quickly.

+ If you have old **family photographs** you want to preserve, why not get them laminated? The lamination prevents them deteriorating further and they can be wiped clean after being handled.

+ When you send a 'get well' **card** to a hospital, put the receiver's name and address on the back instead of your own. That way, if they've been discharged, the card will be forwarded to the patient's home rather than back to you.

+ Wear an oven mitt to stroke **air bubbles** out of clear plastic when covering books or shelves. It makes a tricky job much easier.

+ If you still like to get paper **bank statements**, for an endless supply of personal name and address labels for the backs of envelopes, cut them off the tops of the statements and bills (after paying, of course!) and simply glue in place.

+ The easiest way to get a new **ballpoint pen** to work is to scribble on a pane of glass. It works better than paper, and won't mark the window.

HOUSEHOLD PESTS

ANTS

+ To get rid of ants, sprinkle a little talcum powder around the area where they usually appear.

+ A few drops of peppermint oil on their trail works wonders – apparently ants don't like the smell.

+ A thick chalk line will prevent ants from coming into the house. Draw a line near their haunts and they will not cross it.

+ Plug their entry holes with Blu-Tack. It can be removed and doesn't harm the ants, you or the environment.

+ Keep crumpled dried bay leaves in your cupboards to deter ants.

+ To keep ants out of fruit trees while the fruit is ripe, smear a barrier of Vaseline, about 10cm wide, around the trunk of the tree. It won't damage the tree, but ants won't walk over it and get to fruit.

+ A few mothballs in the toe of a stocking hung in the pantry will keep ants away.

+ Crushed cloves on their route also upset ants.

COCKROACHES

+ For a safe and effective way to get rid of cockroach infestation, clean and wash out shelves and cupboards to remove any eggs, then sprinkle with boric acid, especially in under-sink cupboards.

+ To kill cockroaches and ants, prepare a thin paste of equal parts borax and jam and place in saucers near their haunts. Take care with this mixture and don't leave it where pets or small children can ingest it.

+ Cockroaches will avoid any places that smell even faintly of turpentine.

✳

FLIES

+ Deter flies in your kitchen by growing a pot of mint or basil.

+ Or sprinkle oil of lavender from the chemist on a cloth and use to rub down the windows and doorframes.

+ Or pour a spoonful of lavender oil onto a piece of sponge on a saucer with 2 tablespoons hot water. Add hot water once a day and more oil twice a week.

✳

MOTHS AND SILVERFISH

+ Deter moths and silverfish from your wardrobe by putting a few pieces of dried orange peel in there.

+ Prevent moths and silverfish in boxes or cupboards by sprinkling well with Epsom salts. Add a few cloves for a pleasant smell.

+ Wipe cupboard shelves with cloudy ammonia or lavender or eucalyptus oil to deter silverfish.

+ Place dried lavender in bags in drawers to deter moths.

+ A few drops of turpentine in cupboards and chests will save clothes from moth attacks.

✳

RATS AND MICE

+ The best bait to use on mousetraps is one sultana or a piece of cheese with peanut butter or vanilla essence on it.

Cockroach baits

+

Take a deep round plastic container,
grease the inside with margarine or oil
and pour a little cheap wine or port in
the bottom. The smell attracts the
cockroaches to climb in,
and then they can't
climb out.

OUTDOOR REPAIRS

+ **Guttering** and down pipes should be cleaned at least twice a year
to remove dirt and leaves. When they are hard to reach, use a hose
to flush the pipe right through to the drains. This trebles the life of
metal guttering and stops fibro systems clogging and overflowing.

+ Use a cold chisel to clean out a **crack in cement**, making it wider at
the bottom than at the top. Brush out any chips and pack the crack
with epoxy repair cement. Large holes are treated in a similar way
but you should add a concrete binding agent for extra sticking power.

+ The best tool for **cutting bricks** is a broad-faced cold chisel. Place the brick on a bed of sand and mark the place to the cut with a wax crayon. Place the chisel along this mark with its bevelled edge facing away from the edge to be used. Tap the chisel gently with a hammer to cut a groove across the face of the brick. Turn the brick over and repeat on the other side. Then strike the brick firmly with a mallet until the two pieces come apart cleanly.

+ Remember that **concrete** should never be laid straight onto bare earth: lay a base of sand or gravel first. This will also save on the amount of concrete needed. Pack the base down firmly by wetting with a hose.

+ Cement surfaces can be partially **waterproofed** by brushing with a solution of sodium silicate with a stiff brush. Mix 450g sodium silicate with 4.5 litres water and apply two coats. For best results, apply the coating to the side of the cement where the damp enters.

+ **Cement** should be mixed in the proportions of 1 part cement to 4–5 parts sharp sand. It is important to use sharp sand or the cement will not be strong.

+ **Minor cracks** are no cause for alarm, unless they seem to be getting bigger, in which case you should call in the professionals. Old cracks on windowsills can be simply patched with epoxy repair cement. Loose bricks should be carefully removed, cleaned and replaced on a new bed of mortar, after covering the top and sides of the brick with mortar.

HOME HINTS FOR LESS NIMBLE HANDS

+ If you find it hard to remove twist-off tops from small jars and drink bottles, always have a pair of **rubber gloves** handy for extra grip.

+ Arthritis in the hands can make it difficult to turn **book** pages, but a Post-it note, stuck to the top of the page to be turned, makes it a breeze. Turn the page, remove the note, stick it to the next page, and so on.

+ Paper clips make excellent **bookmarks**. And if you use coloured clips you can clearly mark places you need to turn to often, or quickly, for example in recipe books.

+ If you can't carry things **upstairs** easily, tie a length of cord to a basket and fasten to the banister on the landing. Fill it with what you need and then pull it up and down, as required.

+ If your fingers aren't strong enough to open **ring-pull cans**, slip the handle of a thin wooden spoon through the ring and lever the lid off.

+ If you've lost the end of your **sticky tape**, just rub some talcum powder on the roll and it will show up. And stick a button or plastic tag from a bread bag on the end of the tape when you've finished using it, so it's easy to find next time.

+ If you find it difficult to remove a **cork** from a wide-necked jar, glue a smaller cork to the centre of the lid as a handle.

+ To keep pens, nail files and other small items handy while you're working, place a double-ended **oven mitt** across the arm of your armchair. The two pockets store a surprising amount of goodies.

+ Retrieve a **roller blind** that has flown out of reach with kitchen tongs. It's safer than climbing after it.

INDOOR REPAIRS

+ To re-stick vinyl or lino **floor tiles** that have started to lift, boil a large pot of water and stand the pot on a cloth on the tile for about 10 minutes. The combination of weight and heat will usually re-stick the tile.

+ Small holes in **lino** can be repaired by shredding and melting wax crayons of the same colour to plug the holes. A coat of wax polish finishes the repair job.

+ If you have some spare **lino** for patching, then worn or frayed lino floors can be repaired. First, cut away the worn part with a sharp knife and place this on top of the spare lino, being careful to match the pattern. Use the old piece as a template to cut a new piece, apply glue to the back and press carefully into place.

+ Broken **fly wire** in screens and doors can be mended by darning with fine florists' wire. Don't use knots: just darn a few inches beyond the hole and then cut the wire.

+ Tongue and groove **floorboards** seldom creak but sometimes the odd board works itself loose. A squeak can often be stopped by pouring a little hot soapy water into the cracks to expand the timber. A more permanent solution is to buy some round-headed nails and drive them into the problem board at an angle, into the floor joist, punching the nail beneath the surface of the board. The nails can then be concealed with plastic wood filler.

+ If hand **tool handles** become worn and slippery, buy a roll of tape used for tennis racquet handles. Bind some around the tool handle for a comfortable and firm grip.

+ When **replacing caulking** around a sink or bath, the best product to use is silicone compound straight from the tube. The tube is generally designed so that you can cut the nozzle to give you the thickness of compound you require – cutting close to the tube tip results in a thinner bead, cut further down and you will get a thicker bead. The bead should ideally be a little wider than the gap between the sink and wall. A very wide gap of 5mm or more should be filled with epoxy repair cement for a firmer bond.

+ To repair **chipped grouting** around a sink or bath, remove all the old grouting with a narrow scraper, then brush out with a stiff brush soaked in mineral turpentine. Apply flexible caulking compound straight from the tube to fill the crevice (very wide gaps between sink and wall should be filled with epoxy repair cement).

+ When applying **new caulking** around a bath, to make it last longer fill the bath with water first and climb in while you apply the flexible caulking compound to the join between the bath and the wall. If you do the job with the bath empty, the extra weight of water when the bath is filled will strain the new joint.

+ To fix **loose ceramic tiles**, clear the cavity of all loose dust with a brush or by blowing. Smear the edges only with minimal tile cement and press into position. (If you apply too much cement to the back it has nowhere to go when you push the tile into place; the tile can end up sitting too high off the wall.) When dry, trim off any excess cement with a paint scraper.

+ To repair **loose doorknobs**, remove the bolt from the back of the knob and dab a little silicone caulking compound well away from the exposed edges. Replace the knob and tighten the bolt. If the threads are worn, rub the silicone compound into it before tightening.

+ To tighten a **loose doorknob**, dip it in shellac or clear nail polish and it will reset firmly.

+ Once you locate the source of **dampness** in walls and remedy it, treat the wall with a good fungicide before you try to repaint it. For existing damp stains, remove flaking plaster with a stiff brush and wash the patch with zinc oxide powder mixed to a paste with water. Rinse and dry the patch, then seal with aluminium paint, before painting or wallpapering.

+ To **mend** broken wooden ornaments or delicate china, make a paste of ground rice and cold water and simmer gently until thickened. Paint onto the surfaces, hold together and leave to dry. It will not fail to stick and will last for many years.

+ Alum melted in an iron spoon over hot coals makes excellent **cement** for mending china, glass or metal.

+ For a **tidy workbench**, make a hole in the top of the workbench at one end. Attach a large paper or plastic bag underneath. Brush sawdust and other waste through the hole and into the bag. Remove and empty when full.

+ When the canvas part of a **deckchair** tears away from the frame, machine-sew a wide strip of carpet binding across the canvas and retack into position.

NAILS AND SCREWS

+ To save your fingers from **hammer injury** when driving small nails or panel pins, push the nail through one end of a piece of stiff paper and use the paper to hold the nail in place while you hammer.

+ If you are short of shelf space, store nails and screws by fixing the lids of **screw-top jars** to the underside of a shelf, then screwing jars to the lids so that they hang under the shelf. You can easily see what is in each jar and double your shelf space.

+ When using **nuts and bolts**, the nuts should be an easy fit. Always lubricate the bolt with oil first, and you will find you can turn the nut much further on the final tightening.

+ Screws will go into **hardwood** more easily if you draw the threads across a bar of soap first. The soap acts as a lubricant.

+ Nails being driven into **hardwood** are less likely to bend if you push them through a bar of soap before hammering.

+ Save empty jars of **cold cream** without washing because they are ideal for storing different sizes of nails. The grease residue inside the jars helps prevent the nails rusting.

+ Wood is less likely to **split** if you blunt the point of the nail first – a sharp nail pushes into the timber between the fibres, while a blunt nail cuts into the wood without splitting it.

+ Holes left by large nails can be **filled** neatly by punching them below the surface with a hammer and nail punch. Fill with wood filler and, when dry and hard, sand smooth and finish to match the surrounding surface.

+ If screws, bolts or nuts are **hard to unscrew**, they will often loosen if saturated with eucalyptus oil or white vinegar.

+ To prevent plaster 'crazing' as you hammer a nail into it, first stick a piece of adhesive tape (use sellotape, Elastoplast or masking tape) on the wall in an X shape. Hammer the nail into the centre of the X. If you mark with a pencil on the wall first to show the spot, when you peel off the tape it removes the pencil mark too.

+ When **drilling** a hole in a wall, put an elastic band around the drill at the depth you want to drill to.

+ When you're working with **small nails** or screws, prevent them from rolling about by holding them on a strip of sticky tape, sticky side up.

+ When a **picture nail** loosens, wrap the nail in a little cotton wool, dip it in glue and then replace.

+ For handy **hangers** in the shed, cover nails with empty cotton reels to prevent the sharp edge of the nails cutting into items such as electrical leads or hoses. Use two reels if the nail is long.

LOG FIRES

+ **Pine cones** are great to burn on winter fires as they smell so lovely. If you have an open fireplace, collect pine cones and dry them thoroughly. They will provide you with firelighters in the winter months and a decorative filling for the fireplace in the summer.

+ For an inexpensive and environmentally friendly alternative to **fire lighters**, save all your orange and mandarin peels, dry them on a windowsill in the sun and use them to light your fire.

+ The **white ash** left by a wood fire should be stored in a jar as it makes a good scouring powder for removing stains on metal and china.

BROOMS AND BRUSHES

+ To clean a broom of **cobwebs** or fluff, brush it over the lawn a few times.

+ Brooms and brushes will keep much longer if **washed** occasionally. Soak them for 30 minutes in 2 litres water with 4 tablespoons ammonia added. Rinse and dry thoroughly.

+ If your broom **head** keeps falling off, wind an elastic band around the end of the handle, then push the broom onto the handle and it will hold tight.

+ To repair a **loose** broom head, remove the handle, saw off about 2.5cm of the worn part where it is split by the nail, re-fix the head and nail firmly into position

+ A worn-out broom can be turned into a **floor polisher**. Cut off the remaining bristles to even out the height and nail on a padding of wool. Cover with a piece of velvet, or other thick soft fabric, and lastly with a thin duster.

+ A piece of **inner tube** fixed around the broom head prevents chipping paintwork or knocking furniture while sweeping.

HOME
DECORATING

PAINTING HINTS

+ When painting **stairs or steps** that you need to keep using, paint alternate stairs and allow to dry before painting the ones inbetween.

+ If you are using paint that has formed **lumps**, place an old nylon stocking loosely over the top of the tin and push down with the brush into the paint. This will prevent the lumps getting onto the brush.

+ Save waste by stretching a piece of **wire** across the top of your paint tin. Wipe the brush on this every time you dip it into the paint and the excess will run back into the tin, saving both paint and mess.

+ To avoid a newly painted window **sticking** to the frame, allow the paint to dry and, before closing the window, spray both painted edges with furniture polish and rub gently with a soft cloth. You will find there is no problem with opening afterwards.

+ Scrape hardened paint spots off **glass** with the edge of a coin.

+ To paint a **tin** to use as a plant pot or pen holder, first rub with sandpaper and apply shellac. Be sure the surface is free from grease. After this the paint will stick.

PREPARATION

+ When **washing down** paintwork, if you notice any scuffs or scratches, apply some paint with a cotton bud. It works a treat on small areas and saves cleaning a messy brush afterwards.

+ For best results when painting a **kitchen**, always wash down the surfaces with a solution of sugar soap and water first. This removes the cooking grease that settles on kitchen walls. Then wash again with clean water and allow to dry completely before painting (because it is made of non-drying oils, paint applied directly over sugar soap will never dry properly).

+ Scrape off any **loose paint** from outside woodwork you are going to paint. You can remove the rest with a blow torch. Use the torch in front of the scraper and lift only one strip at a time. Avoid playing the torch on one spot for too long or it will scorch.

PAINTING KIT

+ **Line the paint tray** with aluminium foil. When you've finished, just throw it away. It's so simple and there's no mess. If you have no aluminium foil, use a plastic supermarket bag. Place the tray into the bag, pour in the paint and the bag will sink into the shape of the tray. When finished, just take off the plastic bag and throw it away.

+ Stand your paint tin in an old **saucepan or beach bucket**. It'll catch all the drips and you'll have a handle to hold. A paper plate stuck to the bottom of the paint tin will also collect drips.

+ Keep pieces of card, or paper plates, with your paintbrushes. When you're painting **pipes close to a wall**, slip card behind them and move it up and down as you go. This prevents you marking the wall.

+ For painting **hard-to-reach corners** and other fiddly areas, tack a piece of sponge firmly onto an old ruler and use this instead of a brush. (This is also handy for cleaning and dusting tricky corners.)

+ When **painting a ceiling**, cover any light fittings with plastic bags held in place with elastic bands. Wear a shower cap to keep the paint out of your hair. To prevent paint running down your arms, cut a square of cardboard or foam rubber and cut a hole in the centre. Push the brush handle through this, close to the bristles, to catch any paint drips.

+ If you need to mask an area but don't have any **masking tape** handy, cut strips of newspaper and dampen them. They will stick to the surface for as long as necessary and are easy to remove.

+ When painting window frames, **protect the glass** by smearing with a bar of soap. Any paint smears will wash easily off the glass when the paint is dry.

AFTER PAINTING

+ Clean brushes with turpentine, then warm water and detergent. Add a little **hair conditioner** to the rinsing water – it keeps the bristles soft and supple. Or rinse in diluted fabric softener and then wrap the bristles in kitchen towel. You can also soak the brush in pre-wash soap detergent overnight and follow the above instructions.

+ Plastic paints can be **washed** off brushes under the tap. To remove enamel paints, run the back of a knife from the heel to the tip along the bristles to squeeze out the excess paint, then clean in a solution of commercial paint and brush cleaner (from the hardware store) and mineral turpentine. Store this mixture in a clearly labelled sealed glass jar and it can be used time and time again.

+ Clean paint from your hands by rubbing with **baby oil** on cotton wool – it should come off easily.

+ If you get gloss paint on your hands and have no turpentine handy, rub a capful of **olive oil** into your hands, then rinse off in cold water.

+ To remove paint from **glass**, mix bicarbonate of soda to a paste with cold water, dab on and leave for some time, then rub off.

+ To remove paint from **floor tiles**, wipe with a cloth dipped in nail polish remover.

+ To remove the **smell** of paint, leave a peeled onion in a bucket of water in the room. In the kitchen, add a few drops of household ammonia to a saucepan of water and leave this boiling on the stove.

+ After painting a room, always keep the paint **sample card** in your bag and car, for when you are shopping for curtains, bed linen or towels.

WALLPAPER

+ To **remove wallpaper** from walls, soak a paint roller or sponge mop in warm water and wet the paper thoroughly before scraping.

+ Put wallpaper **paste** in a mop bucket and squeeze out the paste brush in the mop-squeezing section to avoid excess stickiness.

+ When **hanging** wallpaper, stick a bin liner onto your stepladder with masking tape and drop all the wet, paste-covered trimmings straight into it to save on cleaning up.

+ Worn or dirty wallpaper can be **patched** almost invisibly with a spare piece of the same paper. First remove the section and then cut a fresh piece a little larger than the section removed. Tear the edges of the new piece rather than cutting – irregular edges are less obvious to the eye than cut edges. Paste the new section in place.

+ New wallpaper can be hung over old non-shiny paper only if it is in good condition. If not, use a liquid **paper stripper** to remove the old paper – it has strong wetting agents, which go through the paper to dissolve the glue underneath. Allow it to work for about 10 minutes, then peel off the old paper. Score very shiny wallpaper or vinyl all over with coarse sandpaper to allow the paint stripper to penetrate.

+ Protect the wear spots on wallpaper around **light switches** by brushing the area with a coat of clear lacquer. Then you can simply wipe off dirty marks with a damp cloth.

+ Use any **leftover wallpaper** as shelf or drawer liners. Instead of using expensive adhesive shelf paper, buy an 'end of the line' roll of vinyl wallpaper at a sale. Cut it down to shelf size and keep it in place with a smidgen of Blu-Tack. It lasts for ages.

STORING PAINT

+ Store leftover paint in a **screw-top glass jar**. You'll be able to easily see which colour you want if you need to retouch those inevitable chips or scrapes, and the paint won't dry out like it can do in the bottom of a paint tin.

+ Before putting away **unused paint**, smear a little Vaseline (petroleum jelly) around the rim of the tin. The lid will come off easily the next time you want to use the paint.

+ Or, to prevent a tin of **leftover paint drying out**, close the lid firmly and pour paraffin wax around the rim to make it airtight.

+ To **prevent a skin forming** on paint that is being stored, keep the tin upside down – a skin will still form but when you turn the tin the right way up it will be ready to use.

WOOD TREATMENTS

+ When using **varnish**, do not shake the tin or stir the contents first or you will aerate the varnish, giving a rough bubbly finish to woodwork.

+ Make varnish flow more easily by **heating the tin** in a bowl of warm water before you begin. This will take the stiffness out and make the varnish go further, too.

+ All wood surfaces can be **sealed and preserved** with natural timber stain made from three coats of warm linseed oil. Allow 2 weeks between each coat. Thin the first coat with 20 per cent natural turpentine and the second coat with 10 per cent. The last coat should be straight linseed oil.

OUTDOORS

OUTDOORS HINTS

+ If it's raining when you go out shopping, pack an extra plastic bag. Then, when you go into a shop, your **umbrella** can be popped in it – no drips, no nuisance.

+ Also, on rainy days, keep a post tube from the post office in your car. Put your **wet umbrella** into the tube to keep it conveniently out of the way.

+ To **wash your garbage bin**, upend it over a sprinkler and turn the hose on full. Leave it upside down to dry.

+ Save fat after cooking meat or chicken and add equal amounts of honey, bran and pea meal (from health food shops). Press the mixture into a pine cone and hang in a tree with a cup hook as a **bird feeder**. Birds love it.

+ **Beach umbrellas** won't blow away if you weigh them down with a bag of sand. Fill a plastic bag with sand, dig a shallow hole to sit it in and then tie nylon rope between its handles and the spokes of the umbrella.

+ To remove scratches from resin **outdoor chairs**, put some liquid paraffin (from the chemist) on a dry cloth and rub gently. It makes them as shiny as new.

+ To remove oil stains from a **concrete driveway**, pour a little kerosene over the oil and cover it with sawdust. After a few minutes the stain will be absorbed into the sawdust. You can simply sweep the sawdust into a dustpan and add it to your compost. Hose away the residue immediately.

+ Don't throw your old **straw broom** away. When it's too worn down for successful sweeping, cut the straw to a point with a pair of sharp cutters. The broom is now ready for use to clean your large wheelie bin; the pointed part of the straw gets right into the corners of the deep bin without a lot of effort on your part.

+ If you are a golf fanatic, here's a hint for you. Keep two shower caps in the boot of your car. They are a perfect fit for the wheels of a **golf buggy** after a round on a rainy day, to prevent mud and dirt getting into the car.

+ If the vinyl liner of your **pool** is torn, you can repair it – often without draining the water. Many repair materials are designed to cure under water. Obtain a piece of matching vinyl from your pool supplier and bone it over the tear using vinyl solvent and a small amount of the vinyl itself. Apply this glue to both patch and pool wall and press together. This fuses the liner to the wall and gives the patch as strong a bond as the liner itself.

+ Before **shovelling snow**, spray both sides of the shovel with furniture polish – it stops the snow sticking. If you live in a heavy snow area, keep a can of polish in the boot of your car with the shovel.

OUTDOOR ENTERTAINING

+ When eating outdoors, it's easy to **keep flies at bay** without sprays. Simply saturate a cloth with lavender oil and place it in a small tin with a lid. When needed, place the tin in the centre of the table and remove the lid.

+ If you do want to use commercial deterrents, spray a napkin with Aerogard and put it into a glass – the **flies** won't come anywhere near it. Just be careful not to drink from the glass.

+ Before **grilling** food, add 1 cup of cold water to the grill pan. This will make it easier to clean and will also stop fat splattering all over the grill.

+ If you have an old top-loader **washing machine**, keep it to use as an excellent drinks fridge when you're entertaining. The machine is often close to the back door and, when the drum is half-filled with ice, the cabinet and lid provide insulation. The ice lasts for ages and, once melted, the water can be recycled.

Wasp deterrent

+

When eating outdoors, place half a jar of water mixed with 2–3 teaspoons jam, or some beer, several metres away. Wasps and bees will be more attracted to this than they will be to your picnic.

+ To make it easier to clean out the **ashes** of a barbecue, line the base with foil before putting the charcoal in. It will also reflect back heat and keep food warm for a long time afterwards.

+ To work out the fullness of a **gas bottle**, pour boiling water in a stream down one side. The speed of drying will show the line of fullness. You can also test a gas bottle by weighing it before and after you fill it. If you re-weigh it at regular intervals, you should be able to tell how much gas you have left (which means you'll never run out in the middle of a barbecue!).

+ Chasing **paper napkins** is no fun on a hot day. Why not put an umbrella through a roll of kitchen towel and then put the umbrella through the middle of an outdoor garden table. Then you'll always have handy wipes on hand.

+ A nylon shower curtain makes an excellent **waterproof groundsheet** to take on family picnics. It's lightweight to pack and can double as a throw-over if flies are a problem.

FISHING

+ Next time you go fishing, **mark** 10cm intervals along the length of your rod with paint, tape or nail polish. Then you can tell at a glance whether to keep your catch or throw it back for next time.

+ To stop **sand** getting into your reel when fishing on the beach, cut the neck off a small plastic drink bottle and bury the bottle in the sand. Then sit the rod in the bottle to protect the reel.

+ To **scale** fish easily, dip them in hot water for a few minutes.

+ Bottle tops nailed to a piece of wood make an effective fish **scaler**.

+ If you're **skinning** fish, dip your fingers first in water, then in salt. This will prevent the fish slipping.

CAMPING AND OUTDOOR HOLIDAYS

+ To avoid broken ties on outdoor **chair cushions**, place a piece of non-slip matting in the centre of the chair and put the cushion on top. You'll find there is no more slipping or sliding.

+ A tiered fishing **tackle box** makes an excellent first aid kit. Elastoplasts, tweezers, scissors, ointments and safety pins can be neatly kept in the different sections. The kit stays clean, can be locked for safety and is easily carried.

+ Relieve **travel sickness** by chewing a small piece of crystallised ginger.

+ For campers, yachties and caravanners: on a rough or long **journey**, store all bottles that might come to grief in empty (washed) milk or juice cartons. Liquid from a leak will be captured in the carton and a messy clean-up can be avoided.

+ Stop rattles and breakages in the **cupboards** of boats or caravans when you are towing. Empty wine cask bladders make excellent buffers. Simply inflate them to the size you need and use them to pad empty spaces.

+ Buy **sun block** in bulk and decant it into clean recycled roll-on containers. It's easy for children to use at school and on the beach, with far less mess.

+ Eliminate the struggle of getting into a **wetsuit** by slipping a plastic bag over your foot like a sock. The wetsuit leg will slip on easily and then the bag can be removed.

+ Before going away for an extended time, pour a small quantity of **lavender oil** into jam jar lids or saucers and leave them around the house to discourage moths while you're away. It will also lessen the musty smell you often get when a house is locked up.

+ When travelling, tie a coloured ribbon around the handle of your **suitcase**, or stick coloured tape along its sides. Many suitcases look identical, especially when you're tired at the end of a long journey – this will help you locate yours quickly.

+ When camping, if you smear dripping over the bottom and sides of **saucepans** used over an open fire it will make them easier to clean. Rub with newspaper and sand before washing.

NATURAL INSECT REPELLENTS

+ **Plant** pots of mint, tansy, pennyroyal, feverfew, fennel and basil outside where you would like to sit.

+ Melt **camphor** in boiling water and place in rooms overnight. Mozzies dislike the odour.

+ Add a small amount of **Dettol** to ½ cup baby oil in a jar. Shake well, then dab on areas of exposed skin before going outdoors.

+ **Citronella** can be rubbed on the skin to act as an insect repellent.

+ Bicarbonate of soda mixed into a paste with white vinegar will remove the **itch** when applied to bites. This is also good for sunburn. Raw onion juice is also effective for bites and sunburn.

Mosquito repellent

+

Dissolve 2 teaspoons Epsom salts in 1 cup warm water, then wipe over any exposed skin to deter mosquitoes before you go outdoors. It's safe, effective and completely odourless.

CAR CARE

CAR HINTS

+ In near **freezing** weather, put a drop of glycerine on your car key in the evening, then turn it in the lock a couple of times. This will 'oil' the lock and prevent it freezing overnight.

+ On **frosty** mornings, instead of pouring water directly onto a car windscreen, which can quickly re-ice or even crack, place hot water in a plastic bag or hot-water bottle and rub it over the windscreen. This melts the ice and the windscreen won't quickly ice up again.

+ Beat the **summer heat** by keeping a pair of cotton gloves in the car for whenever the steering wheel is too hot to touch if the car has been left in the sun.

+ If you like driving with the windows open but want to avoid **sunburn** on your arms, cut off the sleeve from an old shirt, keep it in the car and slip it over your arm if you need sun protection.

+ To clean bugs off the **windscreen**, scrunch up a plastic mesh bag – the sort you buy oranges in – dip in soapy water and scrub lightly. It is very effective and won't scratch the glass.

+ Always remove tar and grit quickly, as they can scratch the paintwork. Make your own **tar wash** by adding 2 tablespoons kerosene to each bucket of water and wash the car, a section at a time, hosing off with clean water.

+ The easiest way to remove old **registration stickers** is by soaking a piece of cotton wool in nail polish remover and rubbing the sticker until it dissolves (don't let any remover drip onto the window seals or other parts of the car where it can cause damage). Clean the windscreen with methylated spirits before applying the new sticker.

+ When **seat belts** are too hot to touch, slip towelling sports wrist-bands over the buckles. They are easy to put on, take off and wash.

+ When changing a **car tyre**, always loosen the wheel nuts slightly before jacking the car. Never re-tighten the nuts fully until the car is back on the ground, then turn each one a little at a time and in turn. If you tighten each one completely, then go onto the next, the wheels might be out of alignment.

+ A hydrometer is an inexpensive tool to test the charge in your car **battery**. A high reading means a high acid content. A low reading means the battery needs recharging. If it doesn't take or hold the charge, the battery needs replacing.

+ To keep your car **smelling** fresh, store a cardboard pack of fabric softener under the seat. The fragrance lasts for months, and you can still use it as a fabric softener later. Great for linen cupboards, too.

Grease remover

+

Clean oily hands from working on the car by rubbing a generous squeeze of neat washing-up liquid or liquid soap into your hands. Leave it to dry for a few minutes, then wash your hands as usual with soap, rinsing well in cold water.

GARDEN

GARDENING HINTS

+ Paint the handles of **garden tools** with fluorescent or bright paint, so you can easily spot where you've put them down on the ground.

+ Use a pair of food tongs to re-pot cacti or other plants with **prickles**.

+ If don't like getting dirt under your **fingernails** but find gardening gloves awkward to wear, drag your fingernails across a bar of soap before starting. The dirt will then come off easily when you wash.

+ When storing your **gardening gloves**, fold the tops over twice and secure them with a clothes peg to prevent spiders and insects from crawling inside.

+ Spray insect repellent on your **hat** before working in the garden to prevent you becoming a target for flies.

+ An old hot water bottle filled loosely with sand makes a good garden **kneeler** to protect your knees when weeding. Or wrap an old pillow in a bin liner to kneel on. (When you're tired of kneeling, you can use it to sit on!)

+ Save empty plastic seedling pots or small deli food tubs to place over the top of garden **stakes** to protect your eyes when you bend down.

+ When cutting back **perfumed** plants such as lavender, rosemary and scented geranium, strip the leaves onto a tray and dry in a warm dry place. When dried, put them in small paper bags and store in a cardboard box. Drop bags of dried leaves into the kitchen bin to keep it sweet smelling.

+ To heal bent (but not broken) plant stems, **splint** them with matches taped in place with sticky tape.

+ A **trellis**, for a vine or sweet peas, can be an expensive buy, but many builders have off-cuts of steel mesh used for laying concrete foundations. They make an excellent trellis and often cost nothing if you have a friendly builder.

+ When **raking leaves** in the garden in very dry weather, rake them into piles and then hose them lightly. Damp leaves are much easier to handle, you can fit many more into the wheelbarrow and they are easier to transport to the compost.

+ When your plastic garden **rake** is worn out, you can keep the handle to re-use, and stick the rake part upside down in a plant pot – it will make a great support for a small climbing plant.

+ To make perfect gardening tags, remove the top and bottom of an aluminium can and flatten out the can. Cut into strips, press firmly and neatly scratch the name into the soft aluminium. These **weatherproof labels** will never fade or wash off and it is an excellent way to recycle cans.

+ To stop ink on hand-written plant labels smudging in the rain, rub over the writing with a candle to make it **waterproof**.

+ If you're having difficulty turning on **outside taps** that have grown stiff or jammed, here's a simple solution: cut off 5–7cm of old garden hose and slit it lengthways through the middle. Slide it over the tap head, which you'll then find much easier to turn.

+ Hose couplings and other plastic fittings come together **without force** or frustration if the plastic surfaces that touch each other are first wiped over with cooking oil.

+ The proper time to **lift bulbs** to be stored during summer is when the foliage has turned brown. Bulb and stem can be easily separated and the bulb stored. Store bulbs in old nylon tights or stockings and hang in a protected spot during summer. It is possible to see if the bulbs shoot early and they can be planted at once. Unless rains are plentiful in the spring, water the bulbs. This is the time bulbs start to rebuild for the following year and water will provide much needed nutrition.

+ When an umbrella breaks, remove the fabric and tie the frame to a stake. Train a **creeper** over it to make an attractive garden feature.

+ If your **garden soil** is not suitable for a shrub you especially want to grow, dig out a big hole and fill with the right soil mixture. By the time the shrub is well established the roots will be able to live in the natural soil.

+ Stuff barley straw into an old sock and put it into your **pond** to stop algae forming. Take care with this if you have fish in the pond – it is safe in small amounts.

+ Old nylon stockings and strips cut from plastic carrier bags are both excellent for **tying plants** to stakes. They give with the wind a little but will not cut into the stems.

+ To **patch** a bare section of lawn, mow the whole lawn to 2cm and rake up the clippings. Loosen the soil on the bare patch with a hand rake before applying a good-quality lawn seed – add fertiliser to the seed and mix both into the ground lightly. Keep the soil lightly watered and start mowing when the new grass is 2cm or so high.

ATTRACTING NATIVE CREATURES

+ Grow plants that supply a range of foods for native creatures, such as **correas** that flower in winter when less food is available.

+ Low-growing shrubs provide **protection** for smaller birds to move around the garden.

+ A few rocks placed in a garden attract and provide shelter for **skinks and other lizards**.

+ Have shallow dishes of water with stones in the middle in your garden to provide safe drinking water for **bees** and small creatures.

+ Brightly coloured flowers will attract **butterflies and bees** and provide food for the bees, which will then help the plant pollinate. Try lavender, salvia, cosmos, calendula and nasturtiums.

+ To create a **feeding post** for birds, push a slim branch into the heavy base of a table umbrella and then sit it in the garden. Using a branch keeps the birds as safe as possible from neighbourhood cats, as the cat's weight would break it. Attach a wooden tray amongst the smaller, higher branches to scatter with native bird feeding mix.

DETERRING SLUGS AND SNAILS

+ **Shredded paper** makes a wonderful mulch for strawberries and asparagus. The fruit and stems are kept clean, the slugs and snails hate the sharp edges and eventually the paper rots down as compost.

+ Before you plant out flowers and seedlings in **pots and urns**, rub a generous amount of Vaseline (petroleum jelly) around the rim of the container to keep out slugs and snails.

+ To ensure you don't **poison your pets** when using snail pellets in the garden, put the pellets in a small jar and bury it without the lid, to soil level. Only the snails will be able to eat the pellets and your pets will be safe.

+ Or put the pellets in **jars** that are then laid out on their sides — the rain will not wash away your bait, the snails can readily go in and are easily collected.

+ Or cut a hole in the side of an **ice-cream container** (at the top near the lid), put the lid on and some snail pellets inside. Place the container upside down in the centre of your flower bed and the snails will crawl inside.

+ To rid your garden of snails, spread a little **bran** on the ground and cover with leaves such as cabbage or hydrangea. Snails love bran and will congregate under the leaves and can then be easily collected and moved away.

+ If you have a lot of slugs in your garden, plant a **curry plant** among your vegetables or flowers. The slugs will stay clear.

+ Scatter dried crushed eggshells or sawdust around **seedlings** to form a barrier that prevents slugs and snails without the need for chemicals.

+ Plastic drink bottles and cardboard milk cartons make good **collars** for new plants, saving them from slugs and snails, and eliminating the use of commercial sprays, which can be toxic.

RECIPE

Garlic garden spray

+

This will keep insects, snails and
caterpillars at bay. Dissolve 1 tablespoon
grated pure soap, soap flakes or liquid soap
in water. Stir 3 minced garlic cloves into
6 tablespoons vegetable oil. Combine both
mixtures, stir until smooth and place in a
screw-top jar in the fridge. Label clearly.
To use as a spray, add 2 tablespoons
to 2 litres water.

OTHER GARDEN PESTS

+ When fruit on your trees is just beginning to ripen, toss a few strips of silver Christmas tinsel over the branches to **deter the birds**.

+ Place nylon stockings or tights over bunches of grapes when they begin to ripen, to protect from **ants and bees**.

+ If you're tired of having to clean up your garden after neighbourhood **cats**, there's a cheap and easy way to deter them. Cut a few wooden lolly sticks in half, dip the ends in eucalyptus oil, then poke them in around your garden. Cats hate the smell and will stay away. Renew them every couple of months, or after heavy rain.

CUTTINGS

+ Always keep a large pot of good soil by your back door. Then, whenever you have a cutting, you have somewhere to **strike** it. Firm the soil around the cuttings and keep it damp until you are ready to transplant them.

+ When putting cuttings in to propagate, put them in a **plastic container** with holes in the bottom, buried in the soil. This protects them from damage while they develop their roots.

+ To keep cuttings you are **not ready** to plant, place in a screw-top jar with a little water added. Screw on the lid firmly and they will keep for several days.

HANGING BASKETS

+ Old **carpet underlay**, or leftover pieces of underlay, makes ideal liner for hanging baskets. It's soft enough to push into shape and holes can be cut into it to plant seedlings if you want to achieve a ball effect.

+ When potting hanging baskets, put a **plastic shopping bag** between the basket and the liner. The bag helps to retain moisture for the plants, it protects the basket from water damage and prevents soil dropping through.

POTS AND PLANTERS

+ Prevent loss of soil through the **drainage hole** of a plant pot by cutting a circle from an old pair of nylon tights and placing it over the hole before filling the pot.

+ Spread a layer of gravel on the top of **window boxes** to stop soil splashing onto windows and sills when you water. It will act as mulch to help to keep the soil moist as well.

+ When a plant has **outgrown** its pot, only move it up one or two pot sizes. If there is too much soil around the plant, water can miss the roots altogether and the plant will die.

+ Save your coffee grounds or tea leaves (including from inside used teabags) and mix with soil to make cheap **potting mix**. Plants thrive on it, especially ferns.

+ Save used **teabags** for potting a cherished plant. Put the bags under the topsoil and they'll keep the plant nicely moist; if dipped in liquid fertiliser, they also act as a slow-release bag.

+ Use a **shoehorn** to transplant pot plants. It makes an excellent trowel to reach deep into the pot and loosen the plant without disturbing the roots.

+ Old **terracotta plant pots** can be made to look like new again. Remove any dirt with a firm brush, then thoroughly wash them with water and allow to dry for several hours. When they're dry, wipe linseed oil over the outside with a cloth. If the pots still have dry spots after an hour's drying time, apply a second coat of linseed oil.

+ Guttering off-cuts make great **planter boxes**. Turn up the ends to form a box shape – use a heavy block of wood as an anvil and a hammer to form the end around the block. Drill a few holes in the bottom for drainage before screwing to a wall or fence.

+ Or, if you are short of garden space, mount lengths of roof guttering on a moveable wooden frame, in a tiered formation. You will have a **movable flower bed** that can be emptied when you move house – great for renters.

+ Line planter pots or hanging baskets with **fine wire mesh**. This will allow drainage and prevent the soil washing away.

+ Wrap scraps of **raw wool** (from the shearing shed) around the butts of trees and shrubs to prevent curculio beetles climbing up and eating the foliage.

+ An **old wheelbarrow** makes a great plant container: fill it with soil and plant with colourful annuals. You can wheel it around the garden to get less or more sun depending on the time of year.

+ If you are in doubt about the best possible place for a **new shrub**, leave it in the pot for a while. That way you can move it around the garden until you find the ideal spot for it to thrive.

VEGETABLES

+ Melons, cucumbers and beans come up more quickly if they are soaked between layers of **cotton wool** for a few days before planting.

+ When **planting carrots**, mix equal quantities of carrot and radish seeds and sow them together. After a few weeks, the radishes will be ready to pull and eat, leaving the carrots behind, nicely thinned, to mature later.

+ After planting **parsley seeds**, pour a kettleful of boiling water over them and they will germinate in 3 weeks.

+ **Onions** that have begun to shoot in the cupboard can be planted in the garden. In a few weeks, several spring onions should grow from the bulb. Brown onions with the root cut off and placed in good soil will also produce spring onions.

+ Store **onions (or flower bulbs)** from the garden in plastic string bags on wire netting to allow for circulation of air.

+ **Bees** love yellow and purple flowers. Planting marigolds and mauve-flowering plants, such as salvias, around the edge of vegetable garden beds will attract bees for pollination.

+ Plant **brassicas** such as cabbages, broccoli, Brussels sprouts or cauliflower seedlings in the soil that has just yielded a broad bean crop. Beans are a legume and store nitrogen in the soil, which the brassicas love.

+ To reduce **aphids** and disease in your rose garden, plant garlic between rose bushes.

+ **Rotate** crops in your vegetable beds to avoid disease build-up. A good regime to follow is: root crops (carrots, parsnips, beetroot, turnips), followed by legume crops (peas, beans, broad beans), followed by brassicas (cauliflower, broccoli, cabbage, Brussels sprouts).

+ Marigolds, lavender, garlic, basil, sage and rosemary are all great 'masking' plants to grow as **companion plantings** with vegetables – their strong smell masks the scent of the vegetables, confusing insects and keeping them, naturally, away from your crop.

Companion plantings

+

Grow mint, thyme, dill or sage with cabbage, broccoli, cauliflower or Brussels sprouts to ward off white cabbage moth

+

Tomatoes with basil, onions or celery

+

Onions with carrots and lettuce

+

Peas with beans, carrots and corn

+

Potatoes with beans, peas and corn

+

Squash with corn, melons and pumpkins

+

Carrots with beans and tomatoes

+

Beetroot with broccoli, kale, garlic and onions

SEEDS AND SEEDLINGS

+ Looking for a quick way to plant seeds? Put them in a **salt shaker** or spice jar with holes large enough for them to pass through. Then you can sprinkle them onto a seedling tray or over the spot where you want them to grow. It's much easier than sowing them straight from the packet.

+ Watering seedlings from a **watering can** can flatten and kill them. Instead, use a spray gun. It will keep the soil moist and leaves the seedlings upright and healthy.

+ Line **seed boxes** with plastic foam before filling with soil, to help keep them moist and prevent them drying out too quickly. Several thicknesses of newspaper are also effective.

+ Use empty **ice-cream containers** for potting plants. Pierce with a hot steel knitting needle to make drainage holes.

+ When planting seeds in hot weather, cover the box or ground with a piece of **hessian** or a hessian bag until they germinate. Watering through the bag does not disturb the seeds and is more even. Remove the bag at night but keep the seeds covered during the day.

WATER-WISE

+ When planting **new trees**, use a piece of PVC pipe or electrical conduit as a stake, then water directly down the pipe. This saves water and the trees will grow faster.

+ After washing woollens in **eucalyptus wool mix**, put the used washing water in a clean spray bottle and use to spray the leaves of citrus trees to deter aphids and other pests.

+ Next time you change the water in the **fish tank**, pour the dirty water onto your indoor plants. It's an excellent fertiliser that the plants really thrive on.

WEEDKILLERS

+ Pour turpentine on **onion weed** to kill it without harming the environment. Pour it over the green shoots and let it seep into the ground to the bulb. (Never dig onion weed: it just helps spread the bulbs.)

+ To kill weeds on a gravel or paved **garden path**, spray them with malt vinegar you've transferred to a spray bottle. Be careful to avoid any plants. Weeds will quickly disappear and stay away for about 6 months.

+ Pour the **hot water** leftover from cooking pasta or vegetables between the cracks in patio stones and crazy paving. Very hot cooking water (use it immediately) acts as an effective weedkiller. It costs nothing and is kind to the environment.

HOUSEPLANTS

HOUSEPLANT HINTS

+ Keep all your **coffee grounds** to use as mulch for indoor plants.

+ Give your indoor plants an occasional drink of **cold black tea** and they will thrive.

+ Once a month give indoor plants a gentle cold **shower**. This cleans the leaves and gives them a good soaking that lasts for days. If you have an outdoor shower, use that – it will save on mess.

+ Generally, the thicker and more **succulent** plants can do without water longer than thin-leafed plants. Remember to clean the leaves every 2–3 weeks as a plant 'breathes' through its leaves.

+ A few drops of cooking oil, or equal parts of milk and water mixed together, are good for **wiping** the leaves of indoor plants.

+ When potting a plant, place a handful of **foam** pieces with the soil and you won't have to water it as often.

+ For **red spiders** on pot plants, wipe both sides of the leaves with a soft cloth dipped in soapy water.

+ If you have **mealy bugs** in your plants, place mothballs on the soil.

+ Epsom salts helps keep **maidenhair fern** in good condition: sprinkle lightly over the soil after watering.

+ To keep your houseplants healthy while you're on **holiday**, leave them in the bath on top of an old towel soaked in water.

+ Or drill a couple of small holes into the base of an empty plastic **bottle**. Push the bottle into the soil and fill with water. The water will seep slowly out of the holes and keep the soil moist.

CUT FLOWERS

+ Always **cut** flowers early in the morning or late in the afternoon, rather than in the heat of the day. Place them in a bucket up to their heads in water for some hours, or overnight, before arranging. Any foliage with doubtful keeping qualities should be completely submerged for several hours before using.

+ Before you arrange flowers, cut the **stems** under water. This stops air bubbles travelling up the stems and blocking the water flow.

+ A little **salt** in the water will lengthen the life of most cut flowers.

+ When **long-stemmed roses** droop in the vase, stand each one in a wine bottle filled to the neck with cold water and leave overnight in a cool place. Next morning they'll be standing tall once more.

+ Put **carnations** in a vase of fizzy lemonade instead of water. They will last longer and the buds will open.

+ A little **glycerine** in the water will help keep most flowers and evergreens fresh.

+ 1 tablespoon **salt** added to 1 litre water will help begonias, marigolds, bamboo leaves and tuberose last longer.

+ 1 tablespoon **sugar** added to 1 litre water will help asters, daisies, sweet peas, petunias, lupins and chrysanthemums last longer.

+ To take the distinct strong odour from **African marigolds**, add 1 teaspoon sugar to the water.

+ Lilies and gladioli will keep well in water that has 1 cupful **vinegar** added to every 2 litres water.

+ Flowers will keep longer in water in a **stone or pottery** container.

+ If cut flowers refuse to **open**, add some hot water to the vase and the blooms will appear overnight, as will the perfume.

+ **Maidenhair fern** will last longer if the stem tip is burnt and then the fern submerged flat in water for at least 2 hours after cutting and before arranging.

+ **Camellias** carry well when boxed if their stems are stuck in potatoes.

+ To stop **pampas grass** drooping in the vase, spray it with hairspray.

+ Gladioli and roses carry well if each bloom is wrapped separately in damp **newspaper**.

+ Press a ball of **cotton wool** into the base of vases before filling them with water. The cotton wool will absorb all stains from the flowers and keep the vases clean.

Bloom prolonger

+

It's such a pity when cut flowers droop quickly in the vase. Add 1 dessertspoon each of sugar and vinegar to each 500ml water used and you'll find flowers stay fresh much longer.

+ To prevent **camellias** from falling, push a pin vertically up the stem through the base of each flower.

+ A **cracked vase** can still be used for flowers if it is lined with foil. Mould the foil in one piece to fit snugly inside the vase and weigh the base in place. Do not fill above the level of the foil.

+ Cut various sized thin plastic circles from take-away food containers to make **mats** to place under vases, pots and urns to protect furniture and floorboards from being marked.

+ If you have old packs of **plastic drinking straws** you want to use up in the most environmentally friendly way, you can use them (and re-use them) to extend the stems of cut flowers. If the stems are short, and you want to use a tall vase, push the stems into plastic drinking straws until you get the height you want. The straw allows the flower to get to the water.

+ To make a great table decoration, place **white roses** in water containing a few drops of food colouring. The dye will be absorbed by the flower and delightful coloured edges will form on the petals. Use different colourings to suit your home.

+ To keep a special-occasion **flower arrangement** fresh, spray well with water and lay a large plastic bin bag or piece of plastic sheeting gently over the top.

+ To **remove leaves** from flowers or greenery easily and cleanly, wrap a slim strip of scourer around the stem and bring it swiftly downwards. This is an excellent way to strip rosemary stalks, too.

+ Keep pretty **perfume bottles** and carefully remove the spray device. They look lovely holding a single flower – even better when several are grouped together.

DRIED FLOWERS

+ To keep them intact, spray dried flowers, seed pods and grasses with **hairspray** after arranging. This also works on fruit blossoms that drop their petals.

+ If you're disappointed when cut roses don't open, don't throw them away. Put them in the **microwave** on a low setting for a few minutes (checking regularly to prevent over-drying) and you'll have beautiful dried roses.

+ To **dry** flowers, tie in small bunches and hang heads down in a dark airy place until stiff. The darkness helps preserve the natural colour.

+ For flat flowers or leaves for dried-flower pictures, **press** them between sheets of newspaper under the carpet or heavy books.

+ When picking **pampas grass** for dyeing and drying, pick it in full bloom and add a little washing-up liquid to the water with the dye.

NOTES

INDEX

Published in 2020 by Murdoch Books, an imprint of Allen & Unwin

Murdoch Books Australia
83 Alexander Street,
Crows Nest NSW 2065
Phone: +61 (0)2 8425 0100
murdochbooks.com.au
info@murdochbooks.com.au

Murdoch Books UK
Ormond House,
26–27 Boswell Street,
London, WC1N 3JZ
Phone: +44 (0) 20 8785 5995
murdochbooks.co.uk
info@murdochbooks.co.uk

For corporate orders & custom publishing contact our business development team
at salesenquiries@murdochbooks.com.au

Publisher: Corinne Roberts
Editorial Manager: Jane Price
Design Manager: Vivien Valk
Designer and Illustrator: Michelle Mackintosh
Typesetter: Heather Menzies
Production Director: Lou Playfair

Text © Noela MacLeod AO 2020
Design © Murdoch Books 2020

ISBN 978 1 92235 124 1 Australia
ISBN 978 1 91166 808 4 UK

A cataloguing-in-publication entry is
available from the catalogue of the
National Library of Australia at nla.gov.au

A catalogue record for this book is available from the British Library

Printed and bound in Australia by McPherson's Printing Group

10 9 8 7 6 5 4 3 2

The paper in this book is FSC certified.
FSC promotes environmentally responsible,
socially beneficial and economically viable
management of the world's forests.